D1325637

Macmillan, Eisenhower and the Cold War

For my mother

Macmillan, Eisenhower and the Cold War

Richard Aldous

FOUR COURTS PRESS

Typeset in 11pt on 15pt Galliard by
Carrigboy Typesetting Services, County Cork for
FOUR COURTS PRESS LTD
7 Malpas Street, Dublin 8, Ireland
e-mail: info@four-courts-press.ie
and in North America for
FOUR COURTS PRESS
c/o ISBS, 920 N.E. 58th Avenue, Suite 300, Portland, OR 97213.

© Richard Aldous 2005

A catalogue record for this title is available
from the British Library.

ISBN 1–85182–923–7

All rights reserved.
Without limiting the rights under copyright
reserved alone, no part of this publication may be
reproduced, stored in or introduced into a retrieval system,
or transmitted, in any form or by any means (electronic, mechanical,
photocopying, recording or otherwise), without the prior
written permission of both the copyright owner and
publisher of this book.

Printed in Great Britain
by MPG Books, Bodmin, Cornwall

Contents

Acknowledgments

For their help in a variety of ways, I wish to thank Nigel Ashton, Maurice Bric, Peter Catterall, the late Alan Clark, Peter Clarke, Nicholas Crowson, Martin Fanning, Ronan Fanning, Lisa Hoffman, Dan Holt, Alistair Horne, the late Lord Jenkins of Hillhead, Sabine Lee, Charles Lysaght, Mark Lytle, James McGuire, William Mulligan, Phillips O'Brien, Andrew Roberts, Anthony Tierney, Caroline Walsh, Ted Wilson, Sir Oliver Wright, Neville Wylie, John Young, Lady de Zulueta and colleagues in the UCD School of History. Particular acknowledgment goes to the splendid publisher at Four Courts Press, Michael Adams, and to Harry White for introducing us. David Reynolds was an inspirational supervisor at Cambridge, where I first began research on Harold Macmillan. Fellow Macmillanite there Simon Ball has provided excellent ideas and company throughout the intervening years. My wife Kathryn sportingly and lovingly read each draft, watched latterly in bemusement by our daughter. Finally, I dedicate this book to my mother, who, alongside my late father, encouraged and facilitated my every step.

'You must remember, we suffer from a feeble and formal diplomacy, and there has been little real interchange of thought between the English government and foreign powers. You should personally know the men who are governing the world and under circumstances which will allow you to gauge their character, strength and infirmities.'

Disraeli to Lord Salisbury before the
Constantinople Conference, 1876

Chapter One

The road to the summit

AN INTRODUCTION

ON THE FEAST of Corpus Christi 1520, the assembled courts of England and France faced each other at Val d'Or, halfway between Guines and Ardes. Trumpets sounded. Henry VIII and Francis I spurred their horses and galloped forward. Reaching a spear in the ground, they stopped and, still in saddle, embraced.[1] That the warrior-king Henry – descendant of Edward III and Henry V – kissed the cheek of the French monarch was an act of great significance. Europe's oldest and most bitter enemies had come together in a solemn and public way to swear brotherhood. With their kiss came the hope that personal meetings between kings might bring peace and reconciliation where traditional diplomacy had failed. Here, at the Field of the Cloth of Gold, the modern summit meeting was born.

If this meeting of kings was the first summit of the modern period, neither Henry nor Francis would have described it as such. As with so much of political English usage, Winston Churchill coined the word 'summit'. In Edinburgh on 14 February 1950, he made a speech about the cold war in which he called for a heads of government meeting, declaring that 'it is not easy to see how things could be worsened by a parley at the summit'.[2] Churchill used language with care and skill.[3] When he introduced the term 'summit', he knew the image it would conjure up for an electorate about to vote. Relations with the Soviet Union were worsening; the cold war was getting colder and more dangerous. Was Clement Attlee, the grey and school-masterish Labour prime minister, really up to the task of dealing with the Soviets? What was needed, Churchill implied, was a man who could climb the Olympian heights of diplomacy and, god-like, solve the world's problems. Churchill believed he was that man; he had dealt with Stalin before and could deal with him again.[4]

This desire for high-level talks with the Soviets dominated Churchill's thoughts when he returned to power in 1951.[5] Such was his personal commitment to summitry that he was prepared to take his own government to the brink of collapse in order to have it implemented. He met with fierce opposition from within his own cabinet, including foreign secretary Sir Anthony Eden, and also from the Allies. Churchill always maintained that his position was not one of negotiation at any cost but negotiation from strength. The late 1940s had been spent rearming, creating a unitary military structure and strengthening the Western alliance. Now, Churchill argued, the time had come to begin talks with Moscow to reduce the likelihood of war and reach some form of *modus vivendi*. Meetings of Western and Soviet leaders talking on a wide agenda rather like the wartime conferences at Yalta and Potsdam would achieve this. To ensure such meetings took place, Churchill also suggested that he fly to Moscow.[6]

Churchill's summit policy ultimately ended in disappointment. Senior figures – both at home and abroad – did not believe Churchill was physically or mentally up to the task of conducting a personal negotiation (and the memory of an ailing Roosevelt apparently duped by Stalin at Yalta was still too fresh in the collective memory to allow such a situation to arise again).

More significantly, the international situation between 1951 and 1955 forecast against a thawing of cold war tensions. The election of Churchill's wartime associate, Dwight Eisenhower, to the American presidency in November 1952, and the death of Stalin in March 1953, seemed to offer fresh hope for detente. Yet the tensions of the cold war could not be set aside immediately and suspicions remained. Soviet policy reflected the power struggle within the Kremlin itself, blowing both hot and cold.

Ultimately Churchill's policy failed because divisions within the Western alliance made 'negotiations from strength' impossible. The much-trumpeted unity of the Western alliance was itself based on fear of the Soviet threat. Once detente came onto the agenda, it was hardly surprising that the alliance began to unravel. Churchill had wanted a united bargaining position but his policy encouraged discord; it caused damage to Anglo-American relations and fanned the flames of French suspicion that they might once again be left defenceless against a rearmed Germany. Only after West German rearmament was achieved within the context of NATO in 1955, thus alleviating French fears of resurgent German nationalism, were the Western leaders sufficiently united to conduct 'negotiations from strength' with the Soviets.[7]

It was in 1955 that East and West met at a summit meeting in Geneva – it was to be the only time the four wartime allies would meet at a summit until the final signing of a peace treaty with Germany in 1990. By this time, Eden had replaced Churchill as prime minister. Eden, whilst foreign secretary, had been sceptical about the value of summits, but, as Evelyn Shuckburgh scathingly observed, 'when we ourselves are involved, and playing the *beau role*, it is a very different matter'.[8] A great power summit was finally called for July 1955 when Eisenhower upstaged Eden with his 'Open Skies' proposals.[9] The willingness of East and West to talk to each other led to what contemporaries, with echoes of Locarno in 1925, dubbed the 'spirit of Geneva'. The icy hostility of the cold war seemed to be thawing. In that mood, Eden was able to announce a visit to the United Kingdom by Bulganin and Khrushchev planned for 1956 and, when taken with the earlier signing of the Austrian State Treaty, ushered in a new atmosphere of detente.[10]

Before that visit could take place, the new ambience was dissipated in 1956, first, by the manner by which the Soviet Union quashed the Hungarian revolt, and second, by a crisis over the Suez canal.[11] The Suez crisis in particular was a disaster for Britain. On 26 July, Nasser nationalised the Suez Canal, taking revenge for the cancellation a week before by Britain and America of the Aswan Dam project. Eden proposed re-taking the canal by force and, in the face of a dovish US policy, made a covert arrangement with France and Israel for a joint attack. When Israeli troops attacked Egypt, Britain and France announced they would send troops to protect the canal. Their collusion was transparent, and by the time forces arrived in Egypt on 5–6 November, sterling was under pressure, British public opinion divided and international sentiment, particularly that of the Americans, hostile.[12] On 6 November, in return for a guarantee to prop-up sterling, Britain agreed to American demands for a cease-fire in Egypt and, on 29 November, finally resolved to withdraw troops.[13]

Suez was a humiliation for Britain. It exposed the limitations of the Anglo-American 'special relationship' and the precarious nature of Britain's hold over the Commonwealth countries. In the United Nations, the British were denounced as liars and law-breakers. Financially, the American threat to withdraw its support demonstrated the fragility of the British economy. Domestically, Suez was a bitter time as the nation divided for or against the expedition. Friendships were broken, ministers and officials resigned. When the dust settled, it was clear that the tranquillity of the national psyche had been disturbed.[14] On 9 January 1957, Anthony Eden – sick, exhausted and humiliated – resigned from the office of prime minister.

His successor, Harold Macmillan, immediately grasped that this was an opportunity to redefine Britain's role for the post-war world. He also felt the Churchillian hand of history on his shoulder. 'There has been a kind of 1940 spirit', he wrote on becoming prime minister.[15] Moreover, it was to Churchill's model of summitry and personal diplomacy that Macmillan would turn in an attempt to restore the fortunes of the Conservative party at home and British prestige abroad.

*

Until almost the moment it happened, Harold Macmillan was an unlikely choice as prime minister. He had been born in 1894, the third son of Maurice and Nellie Macmillan. He was raised in a well-off, if frugal, environment where financial security came from the immense fortunes of the Macmillan publishing house. He attended Eton and then Balliol College, Oxford, where he was an Exhibitioner. During the first world war, he fought bravely with the Grenadier Guards and was badly wounded. In 1924, he won his first parliamentary seat at Stockton-on-Tees and gained a reputation as being something of a rebel within the Conservative party. Early on, he attached himself to Winston Churchill and it was on his mentor's coat-tails that Macmillan was whisked to power.[16]

Macmillan's background and personal life are extremely important in understanding his behaviour as prime minister. This really amounts to the story of two women. The first woman in his life was his mother. Nellie Macmillan was an Indianapolis widow who had seduced Maurice Macmillan on a trip to Europe and married him in 1884. She was selfish and manipulative, dominating her children in a persecuting and intrusive way. She interfered in their love lives, friendships, pleasures and plans until her death. Nevertheless, it was Nellie who also equipped Harold for his life as a politician. Nervous, sickly and slight as child, Macmillan had instilled into him by his mother a will to succeed that made him a ruthless political operator. She taught him that every adversity could be swept aside if faced up to with courage and tenacity. Nevertheless, whatever he achieved, it was rarely enough to satisfy his mother. She always demanded more, leaving her son bewildered and with a constant feeling of failure. His habit in later life of ingratiation and fawning owed much to this childhood reflex of always wanting to please his mother (and failing).[17]

Macmillan's childhood experiences taught him how to mask his thoughts and emotions. From an early age, his mother demanded compliance, forcing Macmillan to suppress his own feelings. In later life, this was used to devastating political effect; the mask of 'unflappability' would become the Macmillan trademark. He was something like a great actor-manager of the pre-1914 tradition. In his memoirs, Labour's Denis Healey wrote of Macmillan: '[He] was an unscrupulous opportunist and a brilliant actor; his air of Edwardian languor enabled him to get away with innumerable deceptions and political somersaults without ever being detected.'[18] John Boyd-Carpenter, a cabinet minister throughout the Macmillan years, thought that 'he is an actor, to a much greater extent than most politicians'.[19]

Nowhere was Macmillan's ability to mask his feelings more tested than in his dealings with the second woman in his life – Dorothy, his wife. In March 1919, Nellie secured a position for Macmillan at Government House, Ottawa, to serve as ADC to the Governor-General of Canada, the Duke of Devonshire. Within months, he had fallen in love with the Duke's third daughter, Lady Dorothy. She was an 'outdoor' girl of just eighteen and had little time for books or intellectual pursuits. Quite why she was interested in Macmillan is unclear. In all likelihood she was flattered by his attention and lacked the experience to realize just how unsuitable he was. Thus, when Macmillan proposed on Boxing Day, 1919, she accepted. They were married the following year. 'I suppose books is better than beer,' the duke quipped at the wedding.[20]

This union of the bourgeois Macmillans with the decadent Cavendish family was neither comfortable nor happy. Macmillan hated the family's obsession with outdoor pursuits, notably racing. He was fussy, obsequious, earnest and dull. In the light of later events, it is difficult to realise just how insignificant Macmillan appeared to others. His teeth were crooked, his clothes badly cut, his moustache ridiculous.[21] The Cavendish family thought him the most boring man they had ever met and failed to comprehend why the vivacious, if plain, Dorothy had married him.[22]

It was not long before Lady Dorothy began asking herself (and others) the same question. By 1929, she had three children, was sharing a house with her constantly interfering mother-in-law, whom she disliked intensely, and a bed with a man who failed to satisfy her sexually. Although he adored her, Macmillan neglected her dreadfully. He began work at the Macmillan publishing house early in the morning before moving on to the House of Commons where he might stay until the early hours. Left in this way, Lady Dorothy became increasingly bored and took solace in the company of a lover: Bob Boothby, Conservative MP and close friend of her husband. She seduced him and Boothby, never one to turn down a sexual encounter, responded. As it turned out, the affair continued for more than thirty years until her death in 1966. They had wanted to marry but Macmillan refused to divorce Dorothy knowing that to do so would have wrecked his political career.[23]

Macmillan faced this unhappy situation in the only way he knew how: by masking his emotions. His official biographer, Alistair Horne, points out that Macmillan's 'facade of "unflapability" was very much a cultivated defence mechanism. Underneath ... was a great gulf ... of loneliness, and of melancholia.'[24] For the rest of his life, Macmillan would suffer from extreme bouts of 'black dog' depression and a general fatalism. His wife's infidelity was common knowledge and Macmillan himself was regarded as a somewhat pathetic creature (a fact of which he was painfully aware). Only occasionally did the mask slip in public, such as when an onlooker saw him banging his head in despair against the wall of a train compartment. Whatever one might say about Harold Macmillan's life, it was undoubtedly not happy. His sister-in-law, 'Moucher', dowager Duchess of Devonshire, commented with certain insouciance that 'he had a sad lonely life, really'.[25]

During the 1930s, Macmillan was a vociferous critic of Neville Chamberlain (burning his effigy on the 5 November bonfire at his home, Birch Grove, in 1938) and an acolyte to Winston Churchill. With Chamberlain's disgrace came Churchill's hour of destiny, and there, two steps behind, was Harold Macmillan hopeful that his support during the wilderness years be rewarded.[26] He spent two frustrating years as parliamentary secretary to the minister of supply before taking up the more glamorous role of minister resident at the allied forces headquarters in North Africa. Two experiences in this post had a profound influence on his later life. The first was his introduction to General Dwight Eisenhower, allied commander in North Africa. This was a meeting of opposites – Macmillan bookish, nervy and cynical; Eisenhower an outdoorsman, direct and visceral – but the two men formed an excellent working relationship and enjoyed each other's company. In the late 1950s, when both were leading their nations, Macmillan would use this wartime friendship with Eisenhower as the foundation of his foreign policy dealing with the Americans. In was also in North Africa that Macmillan had his first meetings with General de Gaulle, leader of the Free French, and future president of France.

If North Africa introduced Macmillan to the future players of the 1950s, it also showed him the stage on which he wanted to perform with them; it was in North Africa that he gained his first introduction to summit diplomacy. In January 1943, Macmillan attended the Casablanca conference with Churchill. The meeting between the prime minister and President Roosevelt was,

Macmillan recorded in his diary, 'like a meeting of the later period of the Roman Empire' and he christened the two leaders 'the Emperor of the East and the Emperor of the West'[27] Throughout his life, Macmillan had a taste for the sweeping historical analogy; he responded to the Cuban arrival in Angola with the comment that it was 'really Gibbon all over again – as in the fifth century, you never knew when some new set of Ostrogoths were going to turn up in a collapsing Empire'.[28] The idea of emperors meeting to solve the problems of the world would later come to dominate his thoughts on diplomacy.

Macmillan's post-war political life before taking the premiership saw him holding several major offices of state with mixed results. In 1951, he reluctantly took on the post of minister of housing where he initiated measures that were characteristic of the 'Butskellism' of the age.[29] At the 1950 Conservative party conference, Lord Woolton had promised that the Tories would build 300,000 new houses if returned to power. By 1953, Macmillan had surpassed that figure and his own personal prestige soared. In reality, the policy was not, as Macmillan claimed, the transformation of Britain into a property-owning democracy: local authorities had constructed four-fifths of the houses, and many were not new but renovated. Yet the government's expansionist policy clearly satisfied a popular demand for more houses and reflected well on its instigator.[30]

Relative success at Housing was mirrored by disappointment at Defence and the foreign office. As minister of defence, Macmillan, in his own words, 'rather slacked' and was 'a failure'.[31] He stayed there just five months before Eden moved him to the foreign office. In his brief time at King Charles Street he managed to mishandle just about every problem he was given: the Messina conference (where he blew so hot and cold on Europe that no-one – not even his own officials – knew where he stood); the Cyprus crisis during which he rashly proposed 'stirring up the Turks' in order to counter-weight Greek agitation; the bungled naming of Kim Philby as the 'Third Man'; and the British occupation of the insignificant Middle Eastern oasis of Buraimi where he established the principle of non-consultation with the Americans that would end so disastrously at Suez.[32] Contemporaries thought him a disaster, judging that he was Britain's worst foreign secretary since Sir John Simon.[33] After only nine months, Eden moved him to the Treasury. This decision was due in part to Eden's own paranoia about rivals, but Macmillan's manifest incompetence made it easier.

Although personally 'shattered' by the move, it was in many ways crucial to Macmillan's eventual succession to the premiership. For this was the key position he occupied during the Suez crisis, when he was to play a central role. All of Macmillan's political instincts – self-consciously Churchillian – told him to act decisively and damn the consequences at Suez. But 'damning the consequences' was not consistent with his position as the man with his hands on the purse strings during the crisis. As chancellor, he advised on the state of British reserves and the effects that a war might have on sterling. Being a personal friend of Eisenhower, Eden expected him to smooth things over with the Americans. Thus when he said complaisantly that everything on all these fronts would be all right, everyone, especially Eden, believed him.[34]

Positively hawkish before Suez, Macmillan became, in the words of Lord Beaverbrook, the 'leader of the bolters' once troops were engaged.[35] 'First in, first out' was Harold Wilson's memorable characterisation of Macmillan's behaviour.[36] Thus it was ironic that when humiliation and ill health forced Eden to resign, it was Macmillan's reputation as a decisive character that won him the day. His chief opponent Rab Butler, significantly a 1930s appeaser, seemed weak and vacillating. Macmillan, moreover, seemed to possess the right contacts to restore the 'special relationship' along with the bravado to revitalise British morale. Thus when Lord Salisbury lispingly asked his cabinet colleagues

'Well, which is it, Wab or Hawold?' all but one favoured Macmillan.[37] Against all the odds, this nervous but ambitious man with little or nothing to show in the way of real achievement had climbed to the very top of the greasy pole.

Macmillan's position was almost unassailable from the outset. All the talk in the Carlton Club and Smoking Room at the Commons was of a landslide defeat at the next general election. The pro- and anti-Suez factions within the Conservative party saw that retaining power required everyone to unite around Macmillan. Rab Butler pledged loyalty to the new prime minister. In the early days of the administration, if cabinet colleagues attempted to constrain him, Macmillan ignored them, safe in the knowledge that the party had no choice but to rally to his leadership. Thus when Lord Salisbury offered his resignation in 1957 over Cyprus, Macmillan accepted it immediately (glad to take revenge on an old Oxford rival). Three years earlier, the threat of resignation from the same man over summitry had taken the Churchill government to the brink of destruction. Similarly, when Macmillan's complete Treasury team resigned in 1958 over excessive government expenditure, he again accepted their resignations immediately. Such troubles he dismissed as 'little local difficulties'. Nowhere was this ascendancy more marked than in foreign affairs. Macmillan retained the ridiculed and humiliated Selwyn Lloyd at the foreign office, but was, in reality, his own foreign secretary.[38]

At the forefront of Conservative minds, especially Macmillan's, was the forthcoming general election. The odds for victory were long. Labour was consistently ahead in the opinion polls right up to the election day itself in October 1959. Moreover, no party in the twentieth century had won three successive elections. The mandate of the current parliament would expire in May 1960. Macmillan had just over three years to shorten the odds for a Conservative election victory.[39]

On becoming prime minister, Macmillan faced a raft of serious problems that demanded his immediate attention. Britain's world role and how to pay for it, decolonisation, an emergent European Community, a bruised Anglo-American 'special relationship' and the escalating thermo-nuclear arms race were just some of the items on Macmillan's crowded agenda. However, if the problems were daunting, Macmillan also had a sense of this as a favourable moment to consider far-reaching reform. The Suez crisis had provided a salutary humiliation for the ruling elite, initiating a moment of hesitancy and low confidence. It is at just such moments of trauma, when earlier perceived wisdom has failed, that 'change agents' – those policy-makers who wish to challenge the *status quo* – have their opportunity to re-fashion priorities and policies.

It was at this moment that Harold Macmillan stepped across the threshold of 10 Downing Street as prime minister. Leadership had passed to a man of obvious faults and little apparent distinction, yet with seemingly acute perceptions. His life was a sad, lonely one and he was prone to bouts of chronic depression. He had often seemed a pitiful dullard (a reputation not helped by his wife's barely concealed affair with Boothby). In recent years, he had served at three senior ministries – defence, foreign office and Treasury – without accomplishment, and most considered him a man of limited ability. Yet, he had transformed his shabby appearance into that of an Edwardian gentleman, and turned his dull conversation into the driest of dry wit.[40] Whilst holding senior offices of State, he had been one of the few politicians to recognise the significance of the times. 'It is no longer the case', he had commented to Churchill, 'of choosing between the policies of Marlborough and Bolingbroke but of combining them'. He understood that 'external expenditure' had 'broken our backs'.[41] And most importantly, by clambering to the top of the 'greasy pole' of politics, Macmillan had shown a ruthless desire to win.

To clear his mind for the task ahead, Harold Macmillan had 'read a good deal in recent weeks [… and] have now embarked on R.L. Stevenson – which I have not read for very many years.[42] He might have paused to reflect that the journey on which he had started now seemed hardly less perilous than that of Jim Hawkins on his way to Treasure Island, or that along the way he would deal with characters barely more stable than Jekyll and Hyde.

Chapter Two

If you want to get ahead, get a hat

JANUARY 1958–MARCH 1959

'WE SAY TO the Prime Minister', trumpeted the left wing *Daily Herald* in January 1959, 'wake up and seize the chance that now offers for a real effort to make [this] a year of strengthened peace. [...] Now is the time for Britain to give the lead, Mr Prime Minister'.[1] Less than a month later, Macmillan confounded his critics and delighted his supporters by announcing a 'startling and almost sensational event': a personal visit to Moscow to smash through the ice of cold war hostilities.[2]

Popular pressure for direct East/West talks had developed in Britain quite suddenly and with force during the late 1950s. Public opinion polls, increasing in number and sophistication, were gaining a growing influence on the morale and expectations of politicians.[3] By early 1958, the message from the polls was all too clear to Macmillan. Statistics the previous year had indicated that fifty-seven per cent of the population favoured an immediate summit meeting. By mid-January 1958, comparable questions revealed that support for a summit had risen to an overwhelming eighty-three per cent.[4] Compounding the problem was the traditional view of the Conservative party as the party of strong, even bullish, defence, and Labour as the party of detente. The sudden emergence of an influential peace movement made changing this perception more difficult.

Widespread public interest in the nuclear weapons debates during the late fifties followed the development of the hydrogen bomb, one of which might comfortably have destroyed a city the size of Manchester. This added immediacy to the threat of nuclear war that intensified the fear of attack that had afflicted Britain since 1948.[5] Prominent and respected figures such as Basil Liddell Hart had argued in public that Anglo-American nuclear strategy was a 'great bluff' rather than a great deterrent. Both within and outside government, questions were asked about the reliability of American guarantees in an age of mutual nuclear vulnerability. The proliferation of important Soviet targets and the inability of Nato's Strategic Air Command (SAC) to disable them complicated the matter. Developments in ballistic missile technology made the British V-bomber vulnerable on the ground. Advances in the accuracy of surface-to-air missiles increased doubts about the bomber's ability to penetrate Soviet airspace.[6]

The sense of British vulnerability felt within official circles eased when the UK became the third thermo-nuclear power in May 1957, but whatever the strategic realities, public fears about the destructive capability of modern weaponry remained. Public opinion, like Churchill, recognised that the H-bomb was 'as far from the atomic bomb as the atomic bomb itself [was] from the bow and arrow'. It seemed to bring apocalypse one step closer.[7]

In early 1958, these public fears found organised and influential expression. On 17 February at London's Central Hall, the Campaign for Nuclear Disarmament (CND) held its first meeting. More than five thousand people jammed into the main hall and three overflow halls with a further thousand people left on the street. Speakers included prominent Left-wing figures such as Bertrand Russell, A.J.P. Taylor, Michael Foot and J.B. Priestley. The meeting called for the unconditional renunciation of nuclear weapons, an end to testing and the rejection of foreign missile bases.[8]

The popular support that CND attracted was potentially disastrous for Macmillan. Public opinion was crying out for the impasse in East-West relations to be broken and it was the Left that seemed to have the initiative. Macmillan was legally bound to call an election by May 1960, but the Conservatives were well down in the polls. With informed observers predicting a Labour victory, Macmillan had to act quickly to seize public imagination.[9] 'I am said to have lost touch with public opinion in England because I have not already set out for Moscow to see Khrushchev,' he complained in his diary. 'All this is pure Chamberlainism. It is raining umbrellas.'[10]

It was not long before Macmillan set aside his dislike of 'raining umbrellas' as electoral demands suppressed fears about renewed 'Chamberlainism'. Personal diplomacy, particularly a trip to Moscow, seemed an obvious vote winner. As the first year of his premiership ended, Macmillan was ready to take the first steps on the road that would end at Britain's last great power summit in May 1960.[11]

When Macmillan kissed hands on 10 January 1957, there was outstanding an invitation for the British prime minister to visit Moscow. Soviet Premier Bulganin had made this during his visit to London in 1956. Anthony Eden, then prime minister, had accepted the offer and announced he would go to Russia in May 1957.[12] When Macmillan came to 10 Downing Street, the Soviets renewed attempts to bring about a prime ministerial visit to the Soviet Union. The Suez crisis ruptured Anglo-American relations. Harold Macmillan, after his lacklustre performance as foreign secretary, appeared incompetent in foreign affairs. The Soviets hoped to exploit these facts and further unsettle the Western Alliance.

During the first year of Macmillan's premiership, the Soviets attempted to woo the prime minister into visiting Moscow.

Bulganin wrote to Macmillan as early as 2 February 1957 to renew the invitation. A Moscow visit, he suggested, would provide an opportunity for a 'fruitful exchange of opinion on questions directly concerning Anglo-Soviet relations'. He reiterated the case in further letters in April and July. Then a more forthright comment on the subject from the Soviet leader, Nikita Khrushchev, followed. 'We await your prime minister in the Soviet Union,' he declared to the *Daily Express* in December 1957.[13] Given his interest in Churchill's personal diplomacy, Macmillan's initial reaction to a possible visit was surprisingly cautious. On becoming prime minister, he instructed the foreign secretary, Selwyn Lloyd, to decline Bulganin's invitation with 'no reasons and no excuses', but added that he would come when a visit seemed 'timely from the world point of view'.[14]

Macmillan faced something of a dilemma about a possible visit to Moscow. He had a number of constituencies to satisfy. He recognised that an outright refusal would give the Soviets an obvious propaganda advantage. They had made a conciliatory gesture. An unreserved British refusal would appear as unwillingness even to try working for reconciliation. Equally, the Soviets might use a British acceptance to de-stabilise the Western Alliance.[15] Reconciling foreign office advice not to weaken the 'special relationship' with the demands of British public opinion for an imaginative approach to the problems of cold war was not straightforward.

Macmillan gave the first public indication of his thinking in a televised broadcast in early 1958 when he proclaimed a new departure in government policy towards the Soviets:

> There are two ways to preserve the peace of the world and two only – but they are not opposed; they are parallel. First is to maintain full strength of our alliances. There may be some who would seek to open old wounds, to stir differences between us and to incite jealousies. [...] We must

stand together or we shall fall together. But there is a second way that is just as important, the way of negotiation, of conciliation; and don't let's be dismayed by failures up to date. We intend to go on seeking for some agreement with the Russians for disarmament and for the relief of tension in the world. […] We could start by a solemn pact of non-aggression. This has been done before. It would do no harm. It might do good.[16]

Macmillan emphasised the importance of the Western Alliance 'standing together' but, surprisingly, he issued this call for a non-aggression pact without consulting the Americans. The US State Department put this down to the 'non-aggression pact' being an idea rather than proposal, encouraged by a foreign office briefing that Macmillan was just floating a 'trial balloon'. In reality, the proposal had surprised foreign office officials as much as the Americans and represented the opening shots in their struggle with the prime minister's office about the direction of foreign policy, particularly detente.[17]

Faced with yet another prime minister making policy in 10 Downing Street, senior officials at the foreign office resolved to take control at an early stage. A few weeks after Macmillan's broadcast, they made a bid for the high ground in a paper submitted to cabinet in January 1958, entitled 'Relations with the Soviet Union.' It identified 'Communist imperialism' as the principal threat to economic and political stability, arguing that Britain had to strengthen its power and influence in order to counter this threat. The paper continued, however, that Britain was not capable of containing communism alone and must therefore 'work in the closest harmony with the United States'.[18] Above all, Britain should not cause conflict with the USA:

We must keep in step with our allies and in particular with the United States. This observation is not so easy in practice as it may sound. We often form an opinion which is different from that of the United States government as to what points may be worth seriously pursuing with the Russians and the method of doing so.[19]

The rebuke to Macmillan was clear, and the paper's cool attitude on summitry compounded it. Traditionally, the foreign office was suspicious of meetings between heads of government because they complicated traditional diplomatic behaviour. The unpredictable nature of such talks often seemed to exacerbate problems through misunderstanding, spontaneous decisions that could not be kept, or even rash threats. Although 'Relations with the Soviet Union' conceded that the pressure of public opinion meant 'we should reconcile ourselves' to a conference, this did not mean that Britain should make the running in organising such a meeting or pursue a policy independent of the United States.

Macmillan agreed that Britain should not get out of step with the United States, but flatly rejected the paper's position on summitry. The forthcoming election had been in the forefront of his mind since the first weeks of his premiership.[20] Foreign office officials had failed to recognise that Macmillan now saw his electoral chances as inexorably linked with the achievement of detente. As the American embassy perceptively reported to Washington: 'current pressures for East/West talks seem to have developed both suddenly and powerfully in Britain.' [...] This has pretty much become "no. 1" subject in terms of British political and public attention'.[21] To satisfy this public demand for action, Macmillan sought to carve out for himself a role as mediator between East and West – an 'honest broker' between the two hostile superpowers.[22] This commitment to personal diplomacy seemed bound to bring Macmillan into conflict with foreign office mandarins who, like Lord Gladwyn, British ambassador to Paris, 'had always been doubtful about the desirability of "summitry"'.[23]

It was not just the foreign office that had doubts; Macmillan's political colleagues also questioned the wisdom of personal diplomacy. When cabinet decided in 1957 to choose 'Hawold' rather than 'Wab', it placed Conservative electoral fortunes in his hands, but with an implicit understanding that they would sacrifice him if the election were lost. Macmillan accepted this risk readily, because it gave him considerable power. Ministers might question him and even slow him down, but ultimately they would not and could not block his proposals.

Cabinet made clear its scepticism about personal diplomacy at a meeting in January 1958. The foreign secretary, Selwyn Lloyd, explained to colleagues that the prime minister had offered to visit the Soviet Union for discussions about a heads of government meeting. Lloyd recognised an imaginative initiative was needed to break the deadlock on negotiation but argued that a Moscow visit was not the correct way to proceed. 'A proposal on these lines would be likely to provoke anxiety and suspicion among our Allies', he observed, 'and to be interpreted in this country as indicating a weakening in the attitude hitherto adopted by the government'.[24]

Furthermore, Lloyd noted, the home secretary, R.A. Butler, opposed an initiative of this kind. Presented with the firm opposition of the foreign and home secretaries, cabinet endorsed the view that a personal visit to the Soviet Union by the prime minister would be inadvisable. Many had experienced under Eden the consequences of a prime minister playing foreign secretary.

Lloyd had always been unenthusiastic about the value of heads of government negotiations, commenting that 'summiteering is an occupational weakness of any incumbent of No. 10, with the notable exceptions of Baldwin and Attlee'.[25] Yet parliamentary and public derision increasingly eroded Lloyd's ability to resist Macmillan's summit initiatives.

Selwyn Lloyd was not an individual who naturally commanded authority. He was dour in appearance and excited little public or party enthusiasm. Eden had made him foreign secretary in 1955, an appointment generally interpreted as a signal of the prime minister's intention to maintain control of foreign policy. During the debacle at Suez, Eden had refused to accept Lloyd's resignation, but when Macmillan became prime minister, most thought that he would name a new foreign secretary. Macmillan probably kept Lloyd *in situ* because, like Eden, he recognised the benefits of keeping a political weakling at the foreign office. He also did not want to kow-tow completely to the anti-Suez faction in Parliament. Nevertheless, throughout Lloyd's tenure at King Charles Street, the suspicion remained, in the words of one official, that 'we have no secretary of state'.[26]

During an important set-piece foreign affairs debate on 19–20 February 1958, Lloyd's already-battered image suffered a further blow. Tory backbenchers sat in embarrassed silence as the foreign secretary delivered another flustered performance. At the next meeting of the Conservative 1922 Committee attended by the prime minister, their frustration with Lloyd came to a head. One noted unkindly that if the government's case was presented as badly abroad as it was at home, then Britain's national interests were in jeopardy.[27] Press comment was no more complimentary. The *Evening Standard* summed up the general tone when it commented 'our foreign policy appears to be played like a game of Russian roulette. Unfortunately Mr Selwyn Lloyd picks the loaded chamber every time.'[28] In all spheres of political life, Lloyd was condemned as weak, ineffectual and not up to his job. As so often, the cartoonist Vicky best captured public sentiment, suggesting a new best-seller entitled 'Around the World with Nothing On: The Frank Memoirs of Selwyn Lloyd'.[29] The 'emperor' of the foreign office clearly had no clothes.

Like the Soviet foreign minister, Andrei Gromyko, Selwyn Lloyd's mindset was that of the official rather than the politician. In particular, other foreign ministers and diplomats appreciated his calm, business-like manner. However, Lloyd was a sensitive individual. The vitriolic attacks became too much. On 24 February, he wrote to Macmillan offering his resignation, believing that 'the government will do better without me'.[30]

Macmillan would have none of it. 'It is your duty to carry on,' he admonished Lloyd, noting that 'in the old days politics were just as rough as now – if not rougher'.[31] Macmillan was too astute to sacrifice the benefits of having Lloyd at the foreign office. Derided and ridiculed, with no power base in Parliament or Party, Lloyd's position was dependent on the direct patronage of the prime minister. With the foreign secretary beholden to him, it was not surprising that Macmillan should have increasingly set the tempo in foreign policy, particularly summitry. On the same day that Lloyd had offered his resignation, the political correspondent of the *Times* observed:

> Mr Selwyn Lloyd will not cosset and coddle the Commons by allowing one ray of hope to shine feeble warmth upon them without passing it through that prism of disillusion which is the foreign office's long memory. This means, in fact, that he is now lagging far behind the highest echelons in the government.[32]

From springtime 1958, self-interest demanded that Lloyd catch up very quickly.

Even before Lloyd began his conversion to summitry, momentum towards a Moscow visit had been gathering. On 23 January 1958, while Macmillan was away on his Commonwealth tour, Rab Butler answered a question from the leader of the opposition, Hugh Gaitskell, at prime minister's question time about whether a summit meeting might be a good start to negotiations with the Russians. Briefed by Philip de Zulueta, Macmillan's influential private secretary for foreign affairs, Butler answered that 'this is a legitimate point to make because it is contact which matters and results which flow from it'.[33] This statement astonished

Lloyd. 'We have had it,' he gloomily predicted to the American ambassador the following day.[34]

The London embassy, worried by developments in British summit policy, predicted trouble ahead.[35] Two days after his answer in House, Butler met the American ambassador, who expressed concern that Britain seemed to be agreeing to a summit without preparatory foreign ministers talks. Butler, who resolutely denied this, insisted that a summit meeting would only come at the end of a process of negotiation.[36]

Macmillan clarified his own position on pre-summit talks in a speech at Canberra on 30 January. These talks, he argued, should reach agreement on matters of procedure and agenda. This was an unequivocal commitment in principle to a summit meeting, but without detailed discussions in advance on matters of substance. The American embassy in London found foreign office officials to be 'obviously distressed' at this development. Half apologetically, they had told embassy staff that Macmillan was not in frequent contact with London. Staff accompanying him were unqualified to give adequate advice on those matters.[37]

Macmillan's unilateral policy was not only giving distress at the foreign office, but also in Washington. The Soviets had already latched onto policy differences about the summit.[38] By February 1958, the difference of approach on summitry had become a possible irritant within the Anglo-American relationship. The London embassy warned Washington that 'a mood has been created here [...] which could present substantial difficulties in Anglo-American relations unless American policy takes adequate cognisance of these pressures and makes appropriate adjustments to them'.[39]

The Eisenhower Administration had always expressed doubts about the usefulness of summits.[40] The Republican Party had won the presidency in 1952 on a ticket that denounced the Yalta agreements and Truman's 'containment'. It promised instead a vigorous policy of liberation. Republicans used the apparent 'sell-out' on Poland at Yalta as a symbol of Democratic inability to counter the communist threat. Although Eisenhower would use the *New Look* to extend containment to a global scale, his Administration remained suspicious about presidential nego-tiations.[41] Before the president would commit himself to a heads of government meeting, he insisted the Soviets must show practical evidence of their willingness to negotiate. For Eisenhower, a summit would be the means to tie up loose ends after extensive negotiations at foreign minister and ambassadorial level. The Geneva meeting in 1955 had exacerbated his wariness about summitry. He saw the practical result of those discussions as the signing by foreign ministers in May 1955 of the Austrian State Treaty, which had been negotiated in advance. 'Open Skies', only proposed at the summit itself, had come to nothing, as had the so-called 'spirit of Geneva'.[42]

Eisenhower's lack of enthusiasm for summitry was encouraged by Secretary of State John Foster Dulles. He believed communism and capitalism were irreconcilable. Tension between them could not be reduced. Eisenhower agreed with this assessment, often commenting that there could be no real peace until the Soviet system changed internally. He was, however, more aware of the propaganda advantages of summitry than the secretary of state. If some easing of tension could be negotiated, he would happily go to a summit.[43] However, the idea that the only way to do anything was through heads of government annoyed him. After all, he noted dryly, 'So far as I can see nothing good has come out of a conference attended by a president.'[44]

Llewellyn Thompson, US ambassador in Moscow in early 1958, made the formal American position on summitry clear to the Soviets. At talks with foreign minister Gromyko, he made clear that detente could not be achieved at a two- or three-day summit. Considerable preparatory work had to be carried out in advance. Complex areas of disagreement should be discussed at diplomatic level. The American government would only attend a summit meeting when success seemed genuinely possible.[45]

In the spring of 1958, Macmillan believed the most likely area in which progress would be sufficient for the Americans to attend a summit was a nuclear test ban – a subject that would preoccupy him throughout his premiership. The idea of limiting test explosions grew from international concern about nuclear fall-out, especially after the accident following US Pacific tests in March 1954. The anti-nuclear movement started winning public sympathy and a number of leading figures in the West began advocating a test ban as the opening step towards disarmament. Prohibition of tests seemed to satisfy the political requirements of both Russia and America. The US feared that more tests would allow the Soviet Union to reduce the American techno-logical lead whilst the Soviets feared they would allow America to increase that lead. Both superpowers and Britain hoped to prevent the spread of nuclear weapons to other countries, notably France and China.[46] Despite these favourable circumstances, acrimonious disputes about onsite inspections hampered negotiations between 1958 and 1962. A modest degree of success eventually came in 1963 with the signing of the Partial test ban Treaty. Harold Macmillan deserves much of the credit for breaking the cycle of inconclusive negotiation, but in 1958, his motivations were electoral. Dulles recalls Lloyd making this point to him in October that year:

> Mr Selwyn Lloyd took me aside and said that their proposal to agree to a suspension of nuclear testing without regard to other aspects of disarmament was primarily motivated by domestic political considerations. He pointed out that Mr Macmillan felt that this was a very important card to play and that he hoped we would go along with it.[47]

Electoral reality may have driven British policy on the suspension of nuclear tests, but it was hardly likely to capture the imagination of voters on the 'Clapham omnibus'. The conference of experts in Geneva was making little progress. Everything seemed to move so slowly. To convince public opinion that he was breaking the mould on East-West relations, Macmillan needed something more swashbuckling than test-ban negotiations. By the late summer 1958, he was convinced that his earlier idea about a Moscow visit was the only means by which to win over the public. A summit meeting would have been best, but the Middle East crisis of July 1958, which had revived hopes for a summit, had shown that a crisis by itself would not generate the necessary momentum for a meeting. A visit to Moscow might pave the way to a full summit later. In the meantime, as Macmillan confessed in his memoirs:

> A visit from a British prime minister at a period when Britain's power in the world was still formidable and her prestige following the Second world war still undiminished would be no mere conventional courtesy, but rather a startling and almost sensational event. [48]

And a sensational event was exactly what the electorally ambitious Macmillan needed.

*

Despite growing public horror at the spectre of nuclear holocaust, there was something rather theoretical about the threat of a nuclear attack on Britain. Most people recognised the potential for devastation that nuclear weapons possessed, but few believed anyone would be stupid enough to use them. Khrushchev had promised to 'bury' the West, but this seemed a wild bluff. This changed in late 1958 when Khrushchev initiated a new crisis over Berlin. Such an atmosphere was to give Macmillan the opportunity to force past cabinet and the Americans his plan for a Moscow visit.[49]

In the autumn of 1958, the Soviets 'raised the question of normalising the situation in West Berlin' by submitting a formal proposal for 'dismantling the outworn foreign military occupation regime in West Berlin and turning it into a free demilitarized city'.[50] This was a proposal for an Allied withdrawal from Berlin, and a peace treaty between Eastern and Western Germany. Following this, the Soviet Union would relinquish its responsibilities regarding communications between Berlin and the FRG. Having recently declared the Potsdam protocol to be null and void, Khrushchev now guaranteed to maintain the occupation provisions of September 1944 and May 1945 for a further six months.[51] He later explained:

> Our proposal would have legitimatized the provisional *de facto* situation and made it permanent. We were simply asking the other side to acknowledge that two irreconcilable social-political structures existed in Germany, socialism in East Germany and capitalism in West Germany. We were asking only for the formal recognition of two German Republics, each of which would sign the treaty.[52]

The Soviet proposition put the West in an extremely delicate position. As a later British ambassador to the Soviet Union observed:

> If the Soviet government chose to place responsibility for access to West Berlin in the hands of the German Democratic Republic, the Allies could scarcely blockade themselves by refusing to accept German controls. Nor could they go to war because a German official had replaced a Russian. Yet to recognise the German Democratic Republic was to take a step back from the reunification of Germany. To abandon West Berlin, the symbol of resistance to Soviet pressure, was unthinkable.[53]

This echoes the American view. On 13 November 1958, CIA director, Alan Dulles, told a meeting of the National Security Council that Khrushchev's plan created the most complicated situation for the Allies since the 1948 blockade. The purpose of the Soviet initiative was clearly 'to continue pressure on the US and its allies to recognise and deal with the East German regime'.[54]

For the CIA, the Berlin crisis indicated a general hardening of Soviet policy towards the West. Khrushchev was behaving in a way reminiscent of Stalin.[55] The president shared these fears, telling the director that 'he had been worrying late at night as to what the eventual fate of Berlin would be'. That such a situation could arise was clearly the result of the wartime policies:

> He said that in the days when Berlin was divided, when he was not a politician, that he had done his best to make the Americans and British see what a trouble the thing was going to be – but that the political leaders, naming Roosevelt and Churchill had said, 'Oh, we can get along with Uncle Joe'. He said at the time he knew better and that everything he had feared had come to pass.[56]

Eisenhower had always been suspicious of personal diplomacy. The Berlin crisis compounded his doubts. By placing too great an emphasis on personal negotiation, Stalin had fooled Churchill and Roosevelt. The current crisis represented the failure of wartime diplomacy, proving that heads of government were not the people to negotiate deals. Why did everyone want to turn a president into some kind of an 'Alexander or a Napoleon setting up the geography of Europe'?[57]

Across the Atlantic, a similar understanding of the Soviet position was producing a rather different assessment.[58] Macmillan, who desperately wanted to be an 'Alexander or a Napoleon', did not see the Berlin crisis as a warning against the perils of personal diplomacy. Rather, it represented a pretext for a 'startling and sensational event', with or without the blessing of cabinet or the foreign office. The British press, relieved that Khrushchev was not bringing Berlin to a head immediately, urged the Western allies to use the 'six months period of grace' to negotiate.[59] *The Times* demanded the West 'demonstrate that success, not failure, is what it wants', and urged the government to bring 'some imagination' to the crisis.[60] The *Daily Mail* hoped there was 'room for negotiation' but commented uneasily 'Berlin is destined to be written across our hearts at least for the next six months'.[61]

By the autumn of 1958, an interesting situation had emerged within the Anglo-American relationship. Both British and American governments believed that relations with the USSR had reached an *impasse*, symbolised by the Berlin crisis. Eisenhower was increasingly doubtful about the value of personal diplomacy at heads of government level; Macmillan, driven on by public opinion, saw this kind of initiative as essential to his electoral chances. Serious conflict seemed likely. Until September 1959, the British and Americans would wrangle about how to talk to the Soviets. Only two years after Suez, and a year after cabinet had endorsed a policy that emphasised the need for a restoration of stability in Anglo-American relations, Macmillan's policy of detente would put the relationship under renewed pressure.[62]

What mitigated this for the Americans was an understanding about the motivation for Macmillan's proposals. Secretary Dulles called Eisenhower in January 1959, after receiving the British ambassador, to inform him that Macmillan was thinking about a trip to Moscow. 'Of course, he's campaigning,' observed Dulles, adding that Macmillan's 'stock has been going down and today he would have perhaps no more than a 50–50 chance if that much' at the polls. The prime minister had made his proposal because he 'faces an election, probably in the fall, and wants to be the hero who finds a way out of the cold war dilemma, particularly about Berlin'. To this, Dulles recorded, 'the Pres. shotgun reaction is let him go if he is that good'.[63]

Eisenhower and Dulles clearly did not want to reject Macmillan's proposal outright. The president, however, remained pessimistic about the likelihood of success. He 'doubted that they would be able to make a dent in the granite'. Certainly he feared 'the trip would react badly', concluding that 'they will come back with their tails between their legs and then we are smart fellows'. Dulles's main fear was that the Soviets would treat an initiative like this as a 'sign of weakness'. They both reluctantly agreed to tell Macmillan that whilst 'he can call there ... he can't speak for us'.[64]

When Dulles met Ambassador Caccia and offered 'certain suggestions and thoughts for Mr Macmillan's consideration' he could not have made the American position clearer:

> The president and I did feel that a trip to Moscow by the prime minister would be apt to set in motion other direct approaches by the French, the Germans and perhaps others. This would be particularly dangerous at a point when there was as yet no firm agreed position as to how to react to Berlin if the Soviets persisted. I said that we ourselves had abstained very carefully from anything which could possibly be deemed a negotiation about the Berlin situation in our talks with Mikoyan, although no doubt Mikoyan would have been quite glad to be the medium for direct bilateral talks between the Soviet Union and the United States.

However, the secretary of state observed wryly, both he and the president recognised 'a matter of this sort [...] had domestic as well as international significance'.

Dulles had made clear American doubts about Macmillan's proposal and signalled US awareness that the initiative was electorally driven. He had also pointed out that if Britain conducted bilateral talks with the Soviets, then other Western leaders might demand the same privilege. Eisenhower believed that Macmillan's Moscow trip 'automatically raised the question of whether he should invite Khrushchev here'.[66] Macmillan's intention in visiting Moscow was to speed-up the process of arranging a summit meeting but warning signs already showed that the American and French presidents might demand their own photo-opportunities with Khrushchev; the last thing they wanted was to attend a 'Macmillan summit'.

When Macmillan finally made a direct approach to Eisenhower, his pretext for the visit was so transparent as to be ludicrous: he did not want to go to Moscow; his real destination was Washington:

> That is my first objective: to talk frankly with Dulles and the president. […] I think in a curious way the best thing to do would be for me to get to Washington via Moscow. Having been to Moscow it would be natural for me to pay a visit to Bonn […] and Paris […] and neither [Adenauer or de Gaulle] could then complain if we were then to come to Washington because that would appear not as a sign of the intimate Anglo-American friendship of which they are so jealous but in the sequence of an ambulatory prime minister and foreign secretary.[67]

'It looks a little obvious', commented an unimpressed Eisenhower.[68] Dulles agreed and told a clearly embarrassed ambassador Caccia that:

> […] the president felt that this roundabout approach was unnecessary and that if Mr Macmillan wanted to come to Washington and talk with the president about the situation, we saw no reason why he should not do so. We had invited […] de Gaulle so he could hardly complain.[69]

The Americans had seen through Macmillan and, by offering the prime minister an opportunity to visit the US anyway, easily outmanoeuvred him. If he went to Moscow, it was because he wanted to see Khrushchev; there could be no excuses about an 'ambulatory prime minister' who really wanted to come to Washington all along. Macmillan's note in his diary that the Americans 'say in effect they have complete confidence in me and I must do whatever I think is best' is deeply misleading.[70]

Armed with half-hearted American support, Macmillan rail-roaded his plan for a Moscow visit through cabinet in spite of foreign office reservations. Only the foreign and home secretaries knew about the proposal before the Americans. Cabinet had stood in the way of Macmillan's plan one year earlier – he would not tolerate another rebuff. Even senior and trusted figures such as Lord Home, Commonwealth Secretary and later Macmillan's successor, were not told.[71] Cabinet received a proposal that was signed, sealed and delivered. On 3 February, Macmillan informed cabinet that he had approached the Soviets in January about a possible visit and that they had accepted the previous day.[72]

Had cabinet chosen to stop him going, the incident would have caused untold embarrassment to Macmillan personally and been exploited by the Soviets for propaganda. In 1953, a similarly high-handed approach by Churchill had almost caused the government to fall.[73] In 1959, the situation was different. Cabinet had thrown its lot in with Macmillan and, less than eighteen months before an election, had little choice other than to stick by him. Underlying this support was the tacit bargain that Macmillan would get no second chance.

If the way Macmillan dealt with cabinet and the Americans was cavalier, his treatment of European allies was positively off-hand. The question of consultation did not arise. Macmillan informed Adenauer and de Gaulle of the impending visit only two days before the official announcement. This came a full thirteen days after the Americans had been approached.[74] Macmillan's attitude towards Britain's continental allies coin-cided with a period of Franco-German *rapprochement* as de

Gaulle carefully wooed Adenauer.[75] Together they would frustrate Macmillan's summit plans during the following fourteen months.

Anglo-German relations had been strained since Macmillan became premier. Hostile feeling grew in both countries and a number of serious disputes disturbed the good relations fostered by Churchill and Eden. Wrangles over the reductions in troop numbers in Germany implied by the 1957 Defence White Paper, controversy over support costs for the four divisions of British troops there, and the imbalance of contributions in the European Payments Union all served to erode trust. Problems of communication and personal dislike exacerbated these difficulties. Macmillan and Adenauer had little affection for one another. By 1959, Macmillan was denouncing the German chancellor in private as a 'false and cantankerous old man' and 'half crazy'. This problem of communication was not one confined to the prime minister and chancellor. As one German diplomat commented to the *Frankfurter Allgemeine Zeitung*: 'We irritate each other.'[76]

Western allies were not the only ones suspicious about motives for the Moscow visit. Macmillan's offer to visit baffled the Soviets. Britain's relations with Russia had been turbulent during Macmillan's first two years in office. In April 1957, he had received a ten thousand-word letter from Bulganin stating it was 'exceptionally important [that] the present tensions in relations between the Soviet Union and Great Britain should be replaced by good friendly relations'.[77] This was the time of the Aldermaston peace marches, and, with the election approaching, Macmillan had been aware of the need to make a gesture towards detente. However, in 1957, the need to restore Britain's understanding with America hampered his ability to make headway with the Soviets. At Bermuda, in March 1957, Macmillan had signed a Declaration of Common Purpose with Eisenhower that spoke of the need for solidarity against the 'danger of communist despotism'. At this early stage, Macmillan had been unwilling to rekindle American suspicions about British unilateral diplomacy. Relations with the Soviet Union deteriorated throughout 1957–8; first over the Middle East, then Quemoy and Matsu, and finally Berlin. Volatility seemed to be the defining characteristic of Soviet policy and British officials were aware that, when Macmillan flew into Moscow, virtually anything could happen.[78]

The British ambassador in Moscow, Sir Patrick Reilly, went to see foreign minister Gromyko on 24 January and told him of Macmillan's wish to visit. It took the Soviets ten days to make their reply, although this did welcome the proposal. Macmillan's initiative had surprised them, and they concluded it was electorally driven.[79] When asked by Kuznetzov what Macmillan might want to discuss during the visit, the British ambassador had to admit that he had no idea. Much to the ambassador's embarrassment, Kuznetzov simply began talking about the British general election, and at great length. The Soviets knew why Macmillan was coming, and Reilly knew they knew.[80]

Finally, Macmillan was able to make public his plans for a Soviet trip. He expressed the hope to an excited House of Commons that 'our conversations with the Soviet leaders will give them a better knowledge of our point of view and make it easier for us to understand what is in their minds'.[81] The journey was a 'reconnaissance' mission rather than a negotiation. This careless use of language, suggesting to the Soviets that Macmillan was coming to Moscow to spy, was replaced by ambassador Reilly with the more poetic 'voyage of discovery'.[82]

In general, the press welcomed Macmillan's initiative. The supportive *Daily Mail*, which described the proposal as 'the best news of its kind for years', suggested that 'it could mean the biggest step towards a settled peace since 1945'.[83] *The Times* congratulated Macmillan for seeing 'that the time has come when he may seize the opportunity ... to take a positive step in exploring the mind of the Soviet leaders in the course of direct meetings'.[84] Those who harboured suspicions about the prime minister's intentions again found their most eloquent advocate in the person of Vicky. In a cartoon showing Macmillan, Lloyd and Foster Dulles standing next to a graph tracing the fall of Conservative popularity, the prime minister tells the American: 'Why of course my journey's *really* necessary'.[85] Even the left-wing *Daily Herald*, whilst recognising 'the wide assumptions that he is electioneering', praised Macmillan. 'The *Daily Herald* is glad he is going', a leading article commented. 'We earnestly hope he will achieve some good!'[86]

Serious discussion about details for the visit did not begin until mid-February. Macmillan, wanting the trip to be a public relations success, had been concerned by ambassador Reilly's warning to expect 'tough arguing' from the Soviets.[87] The prime minister's obsession with the public relations side of the visit worried foreign office officials, particularly those in the northern department, who feared Soviet attempts to use the election to compromise the British:

> Their basic calculation would probably be that the prime minister could not afford for political reasons to allow the visit to appear a 'failure'. Their aim would be to offer various guises under which it could appear a success at the price of some weakening of allied solidarity. [...] If talks go badly, Khrushchev might try to turn the visit to the disadvantage of the Conservative party.

This was complicated by the fact 'that the visible product ... would [be] almost certainly nothing'.[88] Briefing papers prepared by the foreign office and the chiefs of staff for Macmillan all stressed the need to gauge Russian intentions without entering a negotiation. These papers, particularly that on Germany (whose final draft was written by Hoyer Millar) were deeply conservative. It was only about nuclear tests that the foreign office made any suggestion for meaningful discussion, suggesting Macmillan probe Soviet positions on banning underground tests and limited rights of inspection.[89]

The tame and unimaginative briefing paper on Germany gives no indication of the radical steps Macmillan was planning to take whilst in Moscow. Macmillan had been considering a unilateral compromise package on Germany and Berlin since early 1959. In January, he had posed five questions for foreign office officials, demanding some new thinking:

1. Would the Soviet Union accept a reunified Germany which remained a member of NATO?
2. Would a reunified Germany which remained a member of NATO be compatible with a general detente in Europe including a considerable degree of disengagement by the West and the Soviet Union?
3. What chance is there that after Adenauer's death, Germany would succumb to a Soviet offer to accept the reunification of German territory provided that the reunified Germany left NATO?
4. Could NATO survive effectively if Germany became neutral?
5. If NATO for all practical purposes disappeared, could we, in conjunction with the United States and France, maintain an adequate defence against the Soviet Union?[90]

Sir Gladwyn Jebb, British ambassador in Paris, returned to the foreign office to study the Berlin problem and answer the prime minister's questions. Jebb was an enormously gifted individual who nevertheless lacked either tact or smoothness. He had been a contender to succeed Kirkpatrick as permanent secretary but, as America's London embassy delicately observed, 'the individual qualities and characteristics of Sir Gladwyn would be out of place in the center of a bureaucracy'.[91] These very aspects made him the obvious candidate to find new and imaginative answers to the complexities of the Berlin problem. Moreover, his reputation as a 'loose cannon' guaranteed that more conventional colleagues would be able to distance themselves from his conclusions.

Jebb's thoughts on Berlin were, unsurprisingly, forthright. Britain, he argued, should 'resist all United States attempts to force the issue by military means' in order to 'try to induce the Soviet government to instruct the GDR to assume the functions which it is itself renouncing ... as agents'. German reunification was 'something which we should do our best to avoid' as no 'scheme for German neutrality, even if it were practicable ... would be desirable'. Thus, Jebb concluded: 'though it may not be generally agreed I suggest in my report that ... what we want [is ...] the *status quo* ... more or less preserved'. This conclusion implied that 'coming developments in Berlin are likely to compel the West to give increasing *de facto* recognition to the GDR'.[92]

Two days after Jebb submitted his memorandum to Downing Street, Macmillan issued a directive that the Foreign Office should prepare a plan on European security along the lines suggested by Jebb.[93] As the foreign office was very well aware, this was a departure from the standard Allied position and had implications for allied relationships:

> We should consider at what point it would be possible to reveal a plan of this nature to our allies. There is an almost overwhelming case for the view that we could not bring it out with any chance of its being accepted or being considered as anything but evidence of weak-kneed British unreliability except at the very last moment, e.g. towards the end of a conference with the Russians in May when the negotiations were on the point of breaking down and all the dangers of the autobahn situation were staring us in the face. Then such a plan might be accepted with relief.[94]

Clearly, this was a compromise proposal on Germany and Berlin. Moreover, this would be perpetrated behind the backs of allies and brought into play at a moment of supreme crisis. The reasons for this are evident even from beneath foreign office camouflage:

> The purpose of introducing such a plan would not be because we thought its introduction might be the precursor of a settlement in Europe or would bestow any military advantages on us, but because it could give us certain immediate political advantages. [...] We would gain time (e.g. a further conference in the autumn). Public opinion here ... would welcome it as an easement of tension.[95]

Cabinet remained on the sidelines while officials worked on shaping a new policy position during preparations for Moscow. When they met on 19 February, Macmillan apologised for this lack of consultation, explaining that this was due to his preoccupation with Cyprus. 'Luckily', he remarked high-handedly, 'this does not matter as much as it might – for, as I said at the outset, this is no more than a reconnaissance. We shall be much more concerned to find out what is in the minds of the Russian leaders than to disclose to them what is in ours'.[96]

To most observers Macmillan was apparently going to the Soviet Union with very little to offer. He had no official new proposals or mandates for negotiation. Even Hoyer Millar at the foreign office could only urge him to 'make them show their real views and intentions without revealing what our own real views and intentions may be'. Above all, he advised, Macmillan should 'avoid being drawn into anything resembling a negotiation'.[97] In 1956, Macmillan had wrongly predicted that Eisenhower would 'lie doggo' during the Suez crisis. Three years later he hoped that Khrushchev might play 'doggo' to help Conservative election fortunes; if not, with Gladwyn Jebb's proposal tucked conveniently into his coat pocket, Macmillan believed he had just the bone on which the Soviet leader might chew.

*

Macmillan and Lloyd left for Moscow on 21 February, arriving at 3pm.[98] Shortly before leaving, he had reflected on his political hero Benjamin Disraeli. 'What, I wonder, wd Dizzy do now, if he had to deal with Mr Khrushchev?' he mused. 'How would he play the hand, now that the two giants – USA and USSR – are so powerful?'[99] With a typically Disraelian flourish, Macmillan descended the steps of his Comet IV spectacularly adorned with a foot-high white hat that he had picked up in Finland during the second world war. 'Oh, that wonderful, wonderful hat,' wrote Tommy Thompson, the *Daily Mail*'s correspondent. 'Tall, white, furry and distinguished, it did more for Anglo-Soviet relations in ten minutes than diplomatic exchanges do in a month.'[100] In a sense, this was what the diplomats feared: one misused hat, a symbol of Finnish nationalism and hostility to the Soviets, might well have wrecked months of patient negotiation. In fact, the hat amused the Soviets. In addition, as Macmillan knew, it made a spectacular newspaper image, becoming 'the talk of Moscow and London'.[101] Press excitement was not just about the white hat. Macmillan had embarked on an 'ice breaking mission' for which 'mankind will be in his debt', enthused the correspondent of the *Daily Mail*.[102] Even the usually unsympathetic *Daily Herald* wished Macmillan 'The best of British luck'.[103]

Macmillan's arrival was a 'curiously moving' affair.[104] As he stepped onto Soviet ground, the first British prime minister to do so since Churchill during the war, a military band struck up 'God Save the Queen'. Khrushchev and Mikoyan bounded forward, slapping him on the back in hearty welcome. The rest of the British party, kitted out in Moss Bros. furs, scurried down the steps to assemble on the tarmac. 'We must look either very silly or very sinister,' quipped Sir Norman Brook to press secretary Harold Evans. 'Probably both'.[105]

In his speech of welcome, Khrushchev praised Macmillan for a courageous initiative, reaffirmed his commitment to co-existence, and declared that the talks would benefit the cause of world peace. Towering over the diminutive Soviet leader, Macmillan echoed these sentiments, adding his hope that the visit might 'help to alleviate some of the cares that at present bring anxiety to the world'. Then, with more backslapping and politeness of the 'after you, no after you' variety, the two leaders climbed into the back of Khrushchev's limousine to speed towards the centre of Moscow.[106]

The atmosphere during their informal discussions that day was warm. Khrushchev promised that there were 'no questions dividing them which could not be settled', adding that 'the world [is] now very small and we must do our best to make it possible for us all to live together'.[107] After a sumptuous banquet at the Kremlin Great Palace, Khrushchev accompanied Macmillan and Lloyd to a government dacha at Semyonovskoye where the British party were to spend the night. Alone for the first time, Macmillan began to realise the practical constraints he would face during his visit. The British team knew about the security implications of the visit before leaving London. Rooms (and even trees) were assumed bugged and equipped with two-way mirrors. Private conversation could take place only within the confines of a special 'safe-room' in the embassy, fitted with anti-listening devices. Even Macmillan's private diary remained at home for fear that it might be stolen.[108]

The psychological implication of living in such inhibiting conditions can be guessed at: deprived of the chance to relax and chat, Macmillan would have to live on his nerves throughout the visit with few opportunities to unwind. Anthony Barber, the prime minister's parliamentary private secretary, later commented that Macmillan had found 'ten days without being able to gossip in the evenings with Selwyn and his entourage very galling – it was so much in his style'. The 'bug-proof tent' that Reilly provided at the embassy for conversation proved so embarrassing to Macmillan and Lloyd that, once inside, they felt too self-conscious to talk. In desperation, Macmillan resorted to whispered private conversations on snowy lawns, well away from potentially bugged trees. As he later conceded, it all 'threatened to become ludicrous'.[109]

The casual informality of the first day carried over into the second when Macmillan and Khrushchev engaged in outdoor activities, including clay-pigeon shooting and riding in a troika.[110] Macmillan declined the invitation to go on an elk hunt. He did consent, however, to careering down an ice-mound in a spinning basket with Khrushchev, much to the amusement and astonishment of onlookers.[111] Macmillan, aged sixty-five and recovering from a heavy cold, put on a brave face during the fun and games in the sub-zero temperatures of the Russian winter – weekends at Chatsworth, family home of the Cavendish family, had provided him with years of practice in the art of studied endurance.

When physical exertion gave way to the first informal talks, Macmillan declared his regret that the 'spirit of Geneva' had not led to practical developments. He had come to Moscow to 'see whether it was possible to work out some way of avoiding the dangers which faced us'. Khrushchev replied that the failure of the 'Geneva spirit' was the result of a Western miscalculation. After the death of Stalin, he argued, the West could exploit Soviet internal difficulties to extract concessions. Now the West realised this would not happen, it wanted stalemate. Khrushchev repeated demands that the situation in Germany be 'normalised' with Berlin becoming a free city. If the West refused to co-operate, the Soviets would sign a peace treaty with East Germany. Wavering, Macmillan commented that perhaps 'the establishment of a free city for the whole of Berlin might be considered' as 'a temporary expedient'.[112]

At the end of his first full day in Moscow, Macmillan wrote to Eisenhower to report that 'most of the conversation has been of the nature of friendly courtesies' accompanied by much vodka and caviar. His aim, he told the president, remained unchanged: '[to] probe into their minds a bit, and get some information which may be useful to all of us'.[113] To the deputy prime minister, Rab Butler, Macmillan was more forthcoming about his inkling that the Russians might prove 'more flexible' than anyone had imagined. For the time being, he added, 'I am voluntarily keeping these hopes to myself'.[114]

Macmillan continued to 'probe their minds a bit' at formal discussions with the Soviets the following day at the Kremlin. The question of how to get talks on disarmament started again dominated. Khrushchev made the suggestion that talks should begin at heads of government level, amusingly proposing that they establish first principles before locking up the foreign ministers with a limited supply of bread and water to force an agreement. Encouraged by Khrushchev's talk of a summit, Macmillan told him East and West were not far apart. He thought a summit would be 'wonderful' but suggested that technical preparations should be made first at foreign ministers level first (the standard Western position).[115]

Despite the friendly nature of the talks, Macmillan continued to send gloomy assessments to allies. Writing to Adenauer immediately following afternoon discussions on 23 February, Macmillan noted, falsely, that the meeting had been 'entirely negative' with Khrushchev showing 'no sign of being willing to depart from the Soviet position'. Moreover, he had informed the Soviet leader 'with all the solemnity that I could command that if the Soviet position was as rigid as Khrushchev had described it to me, then the situation was very serious indeed'.[116] Macmillan did not tell Adenauer that he had raised the idea of an all-Berlin Free City without German reunification. De Gaulle and Eisenhower received a similar story of Khrushchev repeating 'all his logic-chopping arguments'.[117] The real problem, Macmillan concluded, was the Soviet's inferiority complex:

From the way in which Khrushchev talked yesterday when we were out in the country, it was borne in on me that in spite of their great new power and wealth, the Russians are still obsessed by a sense of insecurity. The old bogey of encirclement had not yet been layed. Like a poor man who has suddenly made a fortune, they feel uneasy in their new situation and they are resentful and nervous of their neighbours.[118]

Macmillan wrote in such a negative way partly out of a desire not to perturb his Alliance partners, reassuring them that he was taking a tough line with Khrushchev. As Vicky pointed out in the *Evening Standard*, Macmillan was very aware that his 'big brothers' were 'watching' him.[119] Macmillan was also preparing the ground for any possible Soviet concessions later in the visit. If he could represent the Soviet position as intransigent and *still* come away from Moscow with some kind of agreement, this would represent a coup, justifying personal diplomacy. By 'talking up the opposition', Macmillan was ensuring that almost any step forward would be a great achievement secured by his individual diplomatic skills.

Macmillan had already developed a specific timetable for his summit diplomacy that was implicit in everything he said and did during the spring and summer of 1959. By early that year, Macmillan was apparently resolved to fight the general election in the coming autumn and constructed a schedule for inter-national discussion to keep the government in the limelight at home. It all seemed so simple: he would fly to Moscow in February 1959 and then go on to Bonn, Paris and Washington to brief Allied leaders. These trips promised extensive media coverage of 'Macmillan the world political leader' jetting round the globe in a dramatic tireless search for peace. The foreign ministers would meet and talk in the spring resulting in either deadlock or agreement. If agreement were reached, a summit would follow naturally, the next stage of linear progression started by Macmillan's Moscow trip. If the foreign ministers' talks ended in deadlock, Macmillan planned another dramatic intervention by proposing a heads of government meeting to break the stalemate. Either way, Macmillan expected to force a summit by the summer of 1959.

On the evening of the 23rd, Macmillan played host to Khrushchev and other senior Soviets at the British embassy. He spoke of the continued need for co-existence and paid personal compliments to Khrushchev, particularly about his heroic war record (to the Soviet leader's evident delight). The atmosphere was friendly and vaguely drunken, with the Soviets staying late into the night. Macmillan could not have hoped for more. As he later recorded in his memoirs: 'The first three days, therefore, had more than satisfied our expectations.'[120] He hoped to return from Moscow with a Soviet compromise. Talks had been encouraging as the two leaders were developing a certain rapport. Yet, as Don Iddon commented perceptively in his grumpy 'Moscow Diary' for the *Daily Mail*:

> The Iron Curtain is being wrung up so high for the visiting British here that in the opinion of optimists, it may never be wrung down again. Maybe, but I doubt it.[121]
>
> That curtain would come down sooner than anyone imagined.

*

The programme for 24 February gave both sides another rest from serious negotiation. Early in the morning, Macmillan and Lloyd left for the Nuclear Research Institute at Dubna, where the prime minister made a speech. Back in Moscow, Khrushchev was delivering a speech of his own. Harshly critical of de Gaulle and Eisenhower, and positively vitriolic about Adenauer, he denounced a possible foreign ministers conference as 'a bog with no way out' and maintained that only Germans could discuss

German reunification. He then went on to offer the British an immediate non-aggression pact.[122]

The harshness of Khrushchev's speech left Macmillan depressed. Forced again to play host to the Soviets at the British embassy, the strain of the visit suddenly began to show. As the evening progressed, with Khrushchev becoming increasingly boisterous, Macmillan collapsed. Aides rushed him quickly away from the reception to a private room. Feverish, Macmillan lay slumped on a couch whilst the ambassador applied a cold compress to his brow. After a brief return to the reception room, he left for his dacha, worn down by the setback of the day and the physical effects of a lingering cold.[123]

Dejected and at a loss about what to do, Macmillan spent the following morning tramping through the snow with advisers, discussing tactics. Confused and glum, he decided to 'play it by ear', a ploy that left him unprepared for what was about to come.[124] His mood slumped further on reading press reaction to Khrushchev's speech, which correctly reported him as 'shocked' and 'stunned'. The speech had been a 'cold shower' for his hopes and brought East-West relations to an impasse once again.[125] The *Daily Herald* condemned Macmillan for not accepting Khrushchev's request for an immediate summit. 'Obviously there *must* be a summit meeting', it demanded, reminding him that 'the British People want to see the date fixed'.[126] However, it was the *Times* that best summed up the mood of the British press:

> There had been hopes that Mr Macmillan's 'Voyage of Discovery' might let ways forward be seen more clearly after-wards. The speech gives a blunt reminder of the rocks and broken roads, and any new way forward is hard to see [...].[127]

The Soviet delegation, headed by Khrushchev and Gromyko, arrived at Macmillan's dacha for lunch on 25 February with smiles and vodka, which further confused the British party. How was this behaviour to be reconciled with Khrushchev's speech the previous day? At lunch, the drink and conversation flowed freely. As the two leaders settled into their comfortable armchairs by the fire, Macmillan was startled when 'through the haze of cigar smoke and the fumes of alcohol, he [Khrushchev] gave me a wink'.[128] The startled Macmillan wondered what this wink meant, eventually concluding it was Khrushchev's recognition of his schoolboy prank: 'Oh yes, the speech … had been very naughty, but it had been great fun!'[129] Macmillan was fooling himself. Khrushchev's was not the wink of the naughty adolescent but that of the predator. It was not a comment on what had happened but a signal of the aggression that was about to begin.[130]

Exchanges that afternoon were angry and fraught. In a long and rambling opening discourse, Macmillan urged Khrushchev to agree to 'practical discussions' for a summit within the next few months or weeks. He agreed absolutely with Khrushchev that 'it was necessary to negotiate and to take the poison out of the international situation', arguing that 'a settlement could be reached at least on certain main principles and that a determined effort could be made to negotiate'. This could happen only if Khrushchev would drop his Berlin ultimatum. 'All possibilities could be discussed,' Macmillan assured the Soviet leader, but nothing would be achieved except 'by negotiation'. It was 'no use uttering threats or trying to exercise pressure'. The British wanted a resolution of the Berlin question, but it had to come through a conference not 'unilateral denunciation by the Soviet government of their obligations'.[131]

Soviet withdrawal of the May ultimatum was essential for Macmillan. If the Soviets would drop their deadline, the Western Allies would have little alternative but to come to the negotiating table. But why should the Soviet leader make any concession? It seemed clear to him that 'the prime minister had said nothing new today'. The Soviets had made proposals. Khrushchev was 'only sorry that Mr Macmillan had not suggested any'. The West was not proposing genuine negotiation but 'a labyrinth of talk into which a lot of extraneous matters were intended to dragged'. Selwyn Lloyd intervened to accuse the Soviets of issuing a *diktat* on Berlin and threatening the West with war. Who had mentioned war? Khrushchev snapped back. He had never spoken of war in this context; 'It was always the West which was talking in terms of war, […] always speaking about tanks and shooting.' Carry on like this and negotiation would end as 'a conversation between dead people'.[132]

Macmillan later wrote that during these discussions he warned Khrushchev that 'if you try to threaten us in any way, you will create the Third World War. Because we shall not give in, nor will the Americans'. Khrushchev reacted by leaping to his feet and shouting, 'You have insulted me.'[133] Macmillan later admitted that 'we had *all* got rather drunk' before that meeting.[134]

If Khrushchev had been genuinely insulted, he had an odd way of showing it. That evening, he attended a special performance of Prokofiev's ballet *Romeo and Juliet* at the Bolshoi Theatre. He entertained Macmillan to supper during the interval and, for the second half of the ballet, accorded the British prime minister the unprecedented honour of inviting him to the government Box. As Don Iddon observed in his Moscow Diary, 'I was close to Mr Macmillan and Mr Khrushchev in a nearby box and I could detect no sign of coolness between them. Despite the differences, the two men were apparently getting along very well together.'[135]

The *bonhomie* did not last. At discussions the following day, Khrushchev was in belligerent mood. He mocked the British over Suez, personally attacking Eden and Lloyd. He warned Macmillan not to threaten the USSR over Berlin in the way Britain had threatened Egypt over Suez. The Soviets 'intended to carry this thing through', and, if forced to sign a unilateral peace treaty with the GDR, 'would use all the means in their possession to rebuff the aggressor'.[136]

In his memoirs, Macmillan suggested that during this meeting, he kept his temper through clenched teeth, in which case he succeeded in so doing extraordinarily well.[137] Instead of responding to Khrushchev's point, he smoothly re-iterated his call for talks:

> Our aim was to bring about the opening of negotiations and to ensure that such negotiations should be successful. This must be the purpose of all statesmen who see danger. [...] We would think about what Mr Khrushchev had said. We hoped that Mr Khrushchev would also consider what we said.[138]

Macmillan's unwillingness to offer concessions on Berlin was the source of Khrushchev's frustration. He compared the visit with that of the British delegation of 1939, which 'stayed for a month, did nothing and war broke out'. Sir Patrick Dean believed that the prime minister's 'refusal to negotiate' seriously disappointed Khrushchev.[139] Khrushchev had suspected Macmillan's trip to Moscow was an election gambit. Eirenic or offensive, Khrushchev had been unable to push Macmillan beyond bland reiteration of agreed policy on Berlin. Khrushchev was being used, knew it and hated it. In response, he threw a spanner into the works of Macmillan's well-oiled electoral engine to teach the British prime minister a lesson in diplomatic courtesy.

When the two leaders stood at the end of their meeting, Khrushchev announced he would no longer be accompanying the prime minister to Kiev as planned; he had toothache and needed to see a dentist. After all, he wanted his teeth to remain 'sharp and strong'. And with that, he turned and walked out, leaving the British delegation stunned and silent.[140]

'I fucked the prime minister with a telephone pole,' Khrushchev told astonished aides immediately afterwards.[141]

*

Macmillan later described the 'toothache incident' as 'one of the most whimsical diplomatic episodes in history'. In reality, no amount of 'unflappabilty' could hide a humiliating snub. He later noted that because 'my whole purpose was to … lay the foundations for a summit meeting' it was important to avoid a 'foolish and short-sighted reaction' and 'wait upon events'. The reality was somewhat different. Held up to ridicule by the western press and patronised by his allies, Macmillan's nerve broke. Only the urging of Selwyn Lloyd that everything could be smoothed over stopped him ordering his plane and leaving Moscow.[142]

Macmillan's public relations team in Moscow, headed by Harold Evans, had seen the press reaction to Khrushchev's speech and knew this would complicate their task in playing down the toothache incident. 'When in difficulty tell the truth and wear a serene countenance,' mused Harold Evans in his diaries. In fact, this sophisticated manipulator of opinion attempted to pass off Khrushchev's snub with his own brand of Macmillanesque cool. Casually perched on a chest of drawers in the bedroom of his Ukrainian hotel, Evans spoke to assembled journalists (one of whose number was Malcolm Muggeridge, sprawled elegantly on the bed). Evans addressed the pack:

> No, he [Macmillan] was not unduly upset by Mr K.'s deci-
> sion not to accompany him. After all, it had not been part
> of the original arrangements and would have been a very
> unusual courtesy. […] The talks in Moscow had been valu-
> able though it might seem a pity that Mr K. had made this
> public speech it had given the prime minister the oppor-
> tunity to talk about the various matters it raised. He stated
> the Western position frankly and clearly. That was in no
> sense a threat.[143]

Evans' valiant efforts were of little avail. After all, the reporters had the evidence of their own eyes. Macmillan was showing the signs of physical and mental strain, looking 'wan and dejected'.[144] A photograph of Macmillan in the Evening Standard carried the unflattering by-line: 'a tired, somewhat drawn prime minister lights a new cigarette from the butt of an old one as he chain-smokes his way through a press conference'.[145] It was not the image of a man ready or able to accept another term of office. The talks themselves were declared to be 'for all practical purposes, over'.[146] Macmillan had 'little to show' for his efforts: 'The gulf between [both sides] is as wide as ever [and] what is worse, it is hard to see the next stage forward'.[147] 'POOR OLD MAC', carped the *Daily Herald*. 'Mr Macmillan's mission to Moscow is a complete failure.'[148]

As if to heighten Macmillan's embarrassment, Mikoyan publicly denounced the British position on Berlin, accusing Macmillan of ignoring the non-aggression pact that the prime minister had raised himself in 1958. It was the Russian custom, Mikoyan noted icily, 'to begin a meal with tart dishes and end with sweets'; the British had done the opposite. Anthony Sampson, a reporter on the visit, later recalled that 'Macmillan was being made a fool of; the American correspondents looked smug'.[149]

It was a feeling shared by Eisenhower. He wrote to Macmillan of Khrushchev's speech:

> We have become so accustomed to the rudeness of the people in the Kremlin that I suppose that Khrushchev's speech of yesterday, made at a time when you were a guest in his country, should give us little cause for astonishment. Nevertheless, this latest instance of deliberately bad deportment seems to me an affront to the whole free world.[150]

Macmillan had thought his personal charm would break down the Soviet leader. Khrushchev's behaviour had shown this to be a foolish notion, an opinion that Eisenhower had shared with Macmillan before he had left for Moscow.

This put-down from a friend hurt Macmillan. However, what concerned him more was Eisenhower's conclusion about the visit, and the impact these would have on his election prospects. He had hoped the trip might convince Eisenhower that heads of government diplomacy should have an important role in negotiations with the Soviets. Instead, the American president had witnessed a Western leader undergo a brutal humiliation, an unappealing advertisement for personal diplomacy.

Macmillan had understood Eisenhower well. Events in Moscow had confirmed the president's worst fears about the Soviets, personal diplomacy and Berlin. In conversation with acting secretary of state Herter, Eisenhower noted of the Soviets that:

> [he] didn't see how we square this up with their statement that they do not themselves want a major war; said he didn't see how they can go so far and still say they want peace instead of war. [...] president said he begins to wonder what we might do as steps now show we are taking this very, very seriously and not letting it go by default. [...] If this is an ultimatum, we better prepare for it.[151]

Herter agreed with the president's conviction that the West was entering a test of nerve with the Soviets on Berlin. The Soviets might give way right at the last minute, but now war had to be an option. The president was keen to go ahead with 'quiet moves of increasing military preparedness in Europe' and was 'anxious to have atomic weapons moved into Germany as promptly as possible'. The Americans were preparing for the apparently increased possibility of limited nuclear war.[152]

De Gaulle echoed lack of encouragement for Macmillan from Washington. 'We did not expect any really positive results', he remarked. 'These conversations have not been entirely useless because of the impression they have left on you – and which you have conveyed to us of the mind of the Soviet government.'[153]

The value of Macmillan's trip was that of the holidaymaker bringing back some interesting snap shots. 'We told you it was useless trying to talk to them in a civilised way,' de Gaulle and Eisenhower appeared to say, 'but at least you'll have some good stories to tell.' And a moral to draw: that going head-to-head with the Soviet chief could only end in tears.

Macmillan had gone to Moscow for two main reasons: to play the world political leader in an extended party election broadcast and in an attempt to set up a summit meeting for the pre-election period. He had hoped to show it was possible to talk to the Soviets without suffering any indignity or compromise of the Allied position. Nevertheless, although badly shaken by Khrushchev's behaviour and even considering going home, Macmillan quickly recognised that he could manipulate events to his advantage. Khrushchev's 'toothache' made his position as peacemaker seem faintly ridiculous. He decided that, unable to play the role of 'honest broker', he would act, at least in public, the part of a cold war warrior.

Macmillan's allies had all suspected his motives in going to Moscow and thought he was 'going soft' on the Soviets. To recover his tattered reputation in the British press and to convince allies of steadfastness, Macmillan began emphasising his own intransigence. Writing to the American and French presidents on 26 February, he bragged that the talks had left Khrushchev 'disappointed' by British toughness. He had told the Soviet leader that 'since it was no use his thinking that he could force us to abandon our rights or duties he must make up his mind to negotiate in a sensible way'. Khrushchev had 'insulted' Adenauer, and Macmillan 'would not take this lying down since my habit was to be faithful to my friends'. The only point on which he and Khrushchev had agreed was that the situation was 'extremely serious'. It was this tough talking that had instigated the current coolness; a worthy sacrifice if it made the Soviets 'realise the strength of our determination and what is involved'.[154]

Consequent Soviet behaviour gave Macmillan's critique of the situation an air of credibility. Hours before leaving Kiev for Leningrad on 28 February, Macmillan received a personal message from Khrushchev saying his tooth was better and all thanks to a new British drill![155] In reality, the sudden change of Soviet behaviour had less to do with British technology than clever British tactics.

While Macmillan postured as a cold war warrior, his foreign secretary held a clandestine meeting with Kuznetzov in Kiev, at which he told the Soviets that Britain would recognise a separate East German state. Kuznetzov, dispensing with the usual 'poker-face' of diplomacy, expressed amazement at Lloyd's admission: was he really saying that the British would accept a successor state? And what about Berlin? What was the UK's *real* position? The situation in Berlin had reached a crisis point, Lloyd told him, with the likelihood of conflict growing every day. As far as the British were concerned, Russia could sign a separate peace treaty with East Germany but, 'if the Soviet Union wished to create a successor state, they must see that the state carried out the existing obligations [with regard to Western rights]'.[156]

This sensational revelation by Lloyd was the 'British drill' to which Khrushchev ironically attributed the well-being of his teeth; the effect on the Soviets of the surgery was both immediate and obvious. When the British party arrived in Leningrad, Mikoyan and Gromyko unexpectedly greeted them with smiles and courtesy. The Soviet foreign minister soon passed to Lloyd advance copy of a note agreeing to a foreign ministers meeting if the Western powers were not ready for a summit. This was a major concession to the Western position.[157]

Macmillan was ebullient. The Soviets had given him an opportunity to snatch victory from the jaws of a public relations defeat. Apparently humiliated and chastened, Macmillan would have, after all, a prize to take home. Writing to his allies, he pointed out that the Russians had made 'great efforts … to restore cordial relations' and were 'showing us a fairer face since the scowl they directed at us last Wednesday'. Gromyko's note was 'an advance' that proved 'the attitude we tried to maintain of firmness allied with forbearance has paid dividends'. Now the allies must 'refrain from any hasty or too hostile reaction'. There was no mention of Lloyd's conversation about Berlin with Kuznetzov.[158]

The French foreign ministry (Quai d'Orsay) was unimpressed by Macmillan's claims. As early as 26 February, Jean Laloy had told the American embassy in Paris that Khrushchev's speech two days before had been intended as a slap-down for Macmillan and that, having taken an extreme stand, the Russian leader would then offer apparent concessions, which Macmillan would accept to avoid embarrassment. Laloy specifically thought Khrushchev would agree to a summit without agenda and to a fixed-period foreign ministers conference.[159] He complained that Macmillan had rolled-over after a kick by Khrushchev and that the Soviet leader appeared to be 'stealing all the headlines and getting wide public attention for his views on East/West confrontation'. In contrast, 'no strong voices are heard in reply on [the] Western side'.[160]

In Washington, too, the president expressed concern that Macmillan might 'prove wobbly' and would need 'bucking up'. He was showing 'weakness' over Berlin, and the 'bucking up process' would be 'difficult'.[161] Macmillan's plea not to do anything 'hasty or too hostile' confirmed to the Americans that he was overeager to reach agreement.

In the meantime, America continued to prepare for war. The chief of naval operations told the joint chiefs of staff:

> The increased tempo of events surrounding the Berlin crisis plus growing indications that military force may be required to preserve U.S. interests makes it mandatory that the joint Chiefs of Staff re-examine our military preparations.[162]

The following day, two days after the Soviet note offering a foreign ministers meeting, President Eisenhower chaired a special meeting of the national security council that agreed to follow a hard line. There were some harsh words about the British, particularly from vice-president Richard Nixon.[163]

Back in Moscow, Macmillan was winding-down his visit. On his last full day in the Soviet Union, he went to the Kremlin for further talks. These were cordial with both leaders attempting to outdo each other in their praise for the other. Macmillan quoted word for word a translation of a speech given earlier that year by the Soviet leader. In turn, Khrushchev called the prime minister 'courageous' for coming and assured him that the Soviets did not want to 'spread their views by guns and bayonets'. On Germany, he dropped the May deadline and asked the West to name its own date. He hoped that at a bilateral level, Britain and the Soviet Union could now sign a non-aggression pact. This would be 'a show-case to demonstrate that two countries with different economic and social systems were able to make a pact of friendship with one another'.[164]

The proposed pact caused Macmillan some embarrassment. A year earlier, he had called for just such an agreement during a television broadcast and now Khrushchev was offering him one.[165] Macmillan promised to study the document, blustering that 'a treaty of this kind would come more appropriately at a later stage if it could crown a successful outcome of the international negotiations which were to be held later that year'.[166] Both leaders agreed that those international negotiations should form part of a series of conferences. Summit meetings, Khrushchev remarked, should not be 'regarded as a fire brigade to be called out at times of crisis'.[167]

Macmillan was delighted with Khrushchev's agreement to meet at foreign ministers level, proposals for regular heads of government meetings and the dropping of the Berlin deadline. His election strategy, now back on track, was even given a surprise boost by the obliging Soviets who gave him an opportunity to make an uncensored television broadcast. 'This privilege was indeed unique and represented a very substantial concession which I was determined not to abuse', Macmillan wrote afterwards.[168] Consequently it was rather bland, but with enough sound bites to be used at home.[169] Macmillan understood that the television image alone was as important as what he said.[170] Certainly the British press loved it: 'Mr Macmillan made history tonight when he spoke to a Russian audience of at least ten million,' wrote Tommy Thompson on the front page of the *Daily Mail*. 'And what a triumph it was!'[171] In reality, the broadcast probably was seen only by the Communist Party's 'top brass' – few ordinary Soviet citizens possessed a television set. The newspapers carried only brief summaries of the talk. As *Pravda* commented, the whole visit was about British domestic politics. The broadcast was a favour to Macmillan.[172]

On 3 March, Macmillan concluded his visit by signing a joint statement with Khrushchev in the Kremlin. That statement acknowledged differences on Berlin but noted that 'the free interchange of views and ideas which has taken place has created a better understanding of the respective attitudes of the two governments and has thereby made a useful contribution towards the forthcoming international discussions in a wider circle'.[173]

After a brief press conference, Macmillan left for the airport with Khrushchev. With the sun shining from blue skies, it seemed symbolic to the *Times* correspondent that 'the Moscow river, frozen over ten days before, now flows freely'.[174] At the steps to his plane Macmillan warmly thanked Khrushchev for his hospitality and frankness during the visit, declaring in Russian '*vsevo khoroshovo* – all the best!'[175]

As the British Comet IV pulled into the air, Macmillan relaxed for the first time in two weeks. It had been a gruelling and testing time. Khrushchev had humiliated him, but he had accomplished enough since the toothache incident to ensure the trip was a public relations success. Moreover, Lloyd had made the diplomatic point to the Soviets that Britain might be prepared to recognise an East German successor state, which had opened up the way to a summit.

The voyage of discovery was over; now work had to begin on forcing the Allies to meet Khrushchev at a summit. Back in London, the press hailed Macmillan for his courage and initiative, concluding, in the words of the *Evening Standard*, that the prime minister 'has stopped the door from slamming' over Berlin. Hugh Gaitskell, leader of the opposition, must have reflected bitterly on the truth of Illingworth's cartoon in the *Daily Mail*, showing a beaming Macmillan in white hat and furs, the caption offered this simple advice: 'If you want to get ahead, *get a hat*.'[176]

Chapter Three

Staying in the big game

MARCH–JULY 1959

'I**T WAS A** return in triumph', proclaimed the *Daily Mail* of Macmillan's arrival at the House of Commons from Moscow. The Tories stood and cheered, enthusiastically waving their order papers. Even the dejected ranks of Labour MPs could not help smiling at the sheer audacity of this magnificent piece of theatre. There, amidst all the hubbub was the Grand Old Man himself, Sir Winston Churchill. As Macmillan appeared from behind the Speaker's chair, Churchill rose from his bench, with arms outstretched, to beckon the prime minister to come and receive the adulation of his party. For Macmillan, who had ached for so long to be the Churchillian heir, this benediction was a moment of unconcealed delight.[1]

'Nothing was achieved. In all, the results of that visit amounted to the fact that a senior guest had actually come and a meeting had actually taken place. That was all.'[2] This was the unflattering judgement of Soviet foreign minister Gromyko on Macmillan's visit to Moscow. The British prime minister himself was eager to project a rather different view of his trip. With cheers and snorts of approval punctuating every sentence, he told the House of Commons that his Moscow visit had removed the tension from the Berlin situation. The Soviets had withdrawn the deadline in order to negotiate. He concluded:

I made it clear before my visit that our purpose was not to negotiate. It was to try to seek a better understanding of our respective views on these grave issues and the reasons underlying them. This purpose was achieved. [...] The main point is that on these wider problems we reached agreement that the great issues which separate East and West must be settled by negotiation.[3]

Earlier in the day, he had made a similar point to cabinet, reporting that:

The most significant result of these discussions was the fact that the atmosphere of crisis which had been developing in relation to the date of 27 May had been reduced. The Soviet government were now prepared to adjust the timetable, within limits, to the requirements of further negotiations.[4]

To neither House nor cabinet did Macmillan reveal the price he had paid to secure Soviet agreement about a foreign ministers conference: British recognition of an East German successor state.

Macmillan's visit to Moscow had further convinced him of the potential of a summit. In his diary, he reflected that 'Mr Khrushchev is absolute ruler of Russia and completely controls the situation':

Mr K is a curious study. Impulsive; sensitive of his own dignity and insensitive of anyone else's feelings; quick in argument, never missing or overlooking a point; with an extraordinary memory and encyclopaedic information at his command; vulgar, and yet capable of a certain dignity when he is simple and forgets to 'show off'; ruthless, but senti-mental – K is a kind of mixture between Peter the Great and Lord Beaverbrook. Anyway, he is the boss and no meeting will ever do business except a 'Summit' meeting.[5]

Macmillan was confident of his ability to play honest broker at a summit meeting. The more difficult task was persuading his allies to attend in the first place. He set to work on that almost immediately.[6]

Macmillan's talks began in unpromising fashion in Paris. Macmillan noted dejectedly afterwards that 'the French really agree with us entirely over the German problem. But they are trying to pretend that we are weak and defeatist, and that they are for *being tough*'.[7] In meetings with de Gaulle, Macmillan endured long presidential monologues. De Gaulle conceded that only a physical blockade of Berlin by the Soviets would justify war, but admitted he would not say this to Adenauer – it would depress the German chancellor too much.[8]

Macmillan came away from his Paris visit disappointed by de Gaulle's unremitting hard line on summitry. The French president's blatant refusal to tell Adenauer that only blockade would provoke a military response in Berlin made Macmillan's task in Bonn even more difficult. De Gaulle anticipated that the British would bear the bad tidings to a fretting German chancellor.[9]

Macmillan and Adenauer, who did not like each other, found their growing distrust increasingly difficult to hide. Macmillan thought Adenauer, now in his eighties, was too old to be in the job. He considered him difficult, irascible and even a little senile. Adenauer thought that Macmillan was just another British appeaser. The British had appeased Hitler in the 1930s. They now looked set to appease Khrushchev. The chancellor believed that only he stood between Britain and a sell-out to communism on Berlin. These suspicions, predicted the British ambassador in Bonn, 'will not be long in reaching the outside world'.[10]

Macmillan's frank outline of his summit plans confirmed the chancellor's fears. There had to be an early summit, he told Adenauer. Such a meeting should not depend on success at foreign minister level. Indeed, failure at the Geneva foreign ministers meeting would make a full summit even more essential.

It was 'a rather absurd idea to think that only if the foreign ministers passed the preliminary examination could the countries of the world enter for a summit conference'. He had persuaded Khrushchev to drop the May ultimatum. Now, Macmillan explained:

> He could not ask the British cabinet or people to accept a real possibility of war unless every endeavour had been made to avoid this. A summit meeting was an essential part of this work for peace. It was surprising that the British people had maintained as much sense of solidarity with Europe as they had, but unless there was a summit meeting they would be unwilling to face the possibility of war.[11]

With a display of finesse, Adenauer responded that of course there should be a summit with Khrushchev, but with the West in such a weak position was this the right time? John Foster Dulles had recently been diagnosed as having cancer. Was the septuagenarian Eisenhower (wondered the octogenarian Adenauer) 'really up to such a conference or [...] of the calibre required for such a negotiation?' If Dulles had been well, the situation would have been different, 'but it would be a catastrophe for the West if the main country on their side was not able to play its proper part in political negotiations'. At his recent discussions at the president's Gettysburg farm, Eisenhower had been 'absolutely unwilling to discuss any political questions at all'. Neither Herter nor Nixon was 'a big enough figure' to carry the burden. If Eisenhower wanted 'just to speak at the beginning and end of a conference [...] discussion would be difficult'.[12] If these problems were solved, Adenauer concluded, he would happily accept an August summit, even offering to take the matter up with the French. Spectacularly missing the point, Macmillan latched on to this last comment, noting in his diary: 'It is such a great thing to have got such complete agreement with the Germans.'[13]

When speaking to Eisenhower in January of his proposed Moscow visit, Macmillan had presented it as the best way to get to Washington. Unlikely as that seemed, Britain's 'ambulatory prime minister' finally arrived for talks in Washington in the middle of March to tell Eisenhower that he would not 'face the really grave decisions of peace and war until there has been a summit meeting'.[14]

Eisenhower understood Macmillan's position but recognised that America had options beyond the simplistic choice between a Four Power summit and war. Prominent among these options was direct talks with Khrushchev at a superpower summit. Ironically, it was Macmillan's visit to Moscow that provided a green light for bilateral talks with the Soviet Union. Macmillan was in no position to deny the American president talks along the lines of those he had already conducted himself.[15]

Eisenhower's growing sympathy towards the idea of personal talks with Khrushchev was a change in thinking that coincided with the demise of John Foster Dulles. The secretary's health was declining rapidly. His influence on the president was diminishing. Dulles disliked summitry, but from his hospital bed was unable to stop the president's thoughts from turning to his place in history. Eisenhower, like Churchill, wanted to be remembered as a great peacemaker as well as a great warrior. His term of office would end in January 1961. His real powers would have dwindled by Labor Day 1960 when the presidential election campaign was to begin. With so little time left, and Macmillan pushing his own claims as the 'dove' of the Western Alliance, Eisenhower began to look at ways to launch his own bid for détente.[16]

With the British party already in Washington, Eisenhower warned Herter that he 'might startle Macmillan a little by saying now that he has seen Khrushchev, [and ...] is thinking of asking Khrushchev to come here'. If the foreign ministers meeting was 'completely negative then he would go to bilateral talks'.[17] General Andrew Goodpaster, Eisenhower's staff secretary and closest personal adviser, had already told Herter of the president's fears that 'if there was no progress at all and it was clear from the foreign ministers meeting that there was no prospect for progress at a summit meeting, the president would be subject to impeachment if he agreed to a summit meeting'.[18]

When Eisenhower met Herter and Goodpaster on 14 March, he admitted frankly that progress was an 'almost undefinable term'. The reality was that the foreign ministers could do little more than set down 'the areas of agreement and particularly the points of difference which the heads of government would have to negotiate'. If this could be achieved in Geneva, enough scope would remain for the president to invite Khrushchev to the US well before any summit meeting.[19]

Macmillan's glory seeking – his desire to be 'the hero who finds a way out of the cold war' – clearly bothered Eisenhower.[20] Why should he help Macmillan with his election when in 1956 the Conservatives had cared so little about helping Eisenhower?[21] To make matters worse, the British press now proclaimed Macmillan as the true leader of the Western world, which allowed US Democrats to contrast his Moscow initiative with the president's apparent inactivity.[22] Eisenhower was uneasy about Macmillan's motives, believing there was 'something behind all this, even more than Macmillan's political ambitions and his forthcoming election'. Whatever game Macmillan was playing, it was time to give him a 'jolt'. Hints about bilateral talks with the Soviets were just the way to do it. Let's give him a 'real snarl', Eisenhower concluded.[23]

At Camp David, the president's mountain retreat, the two leaders were genuinely intimate and gossipy, watching Westerns and chatting about the old days in North Africa. When it came to discussing the summit, however, the exchanges were heated and angry with 'snarling' on both sides. This came to a head during a row before dinner at which, according to Goodpaster, both men 'expressed themselves most powerfully'. Macmillan launched into a tirade against American unwillingness to set a date for a summit, bluntly telling Eisenhower that:

> The British people will not go to war over this matter [Berlin] without having had a prior summit meeting. Eight Thermo-nuclear weapons, which ... the Soviets could deliver against England, would destroy [our] country and kill 20 million people. [...] Even if we reach no agreement, such a meeting [is] a necessary step.[24]

Both remembered the 1948 Berlin airlift and recognised the spectre of war as a fearsome reality.[25] If Eisenhower would not agree to an early summit, threatened Macmillan, he would have no alternative but to send his own note to Khrushchev outlining his own willingness.[26]

Eisenhower's response made it clear that Macmillan had over-stepped the mark. His temper rising, Eisenhower reminded the prime minister that 'the American people must also be considered in this matter':

> They too have strong views. He had put the matter to them on the basis of going to a summit meeting only if developments so justify and he did not intend to change this position. We also are aware ... that we might have casualties in war of the order of 70 million people. While others could talk about going to a summit meeting under threat of attack by the Soviets, he for one would not attend and they could hold their summit meeting without him.[27]

Playing his First World War theme, Macmillan urged the president to remember that if Sir Edward Grey had travelled to a summit rather than gone fishing, war might have been avoided in 1914.[28] Eisenhower retorted that 'prior to world war two, Neville Chamberlain went to such a meeting and it is not the kind of meeting with which he intends to be associated'.[29] If Eisenhower intended to 'jolt' Macmillan, calling him an appeaser had the desired effect.

Back in London, a disaffected Macmillan reflected on the failure of his diplomacy in the three western capitals. 'How Mr Khrushchev must laugh at us all!' he recorded angrily in his diary. 'It is all rather sad. [...] De Gaulle and Adenauer are just hopeless [...] De Gaulle will not play with me or anyone else. Adenauer is now half crazy ... Eisenhower is hesitant and unsure of himself.'[30]

The ebullient optimism about a pre-election summit, which had gripped Macmillan on his return from Moscow, had faded. It was going to be a difficult summer.

*

The behaviour of alliance partners disappointed Macmillan but he could take heart from opinion polls that suggested public support for his globetrotting diplomacy.[31] Gallup polls recorded general support for Macmillan's summit policy with fifty-one per cent of those questioned believing the prime minister had 'achieved something' in Moscow. When asked 'in general, do you approve or disapprove of the way the government is handling foreign affairs?' Forty-four per cent approved, an increase of ten percentage points on the previous month.[32]

Buoyed-up by the rapidly improving poll ratings, Conservative MPs began urging the prime minister to call a snap general election to cash-in on his popularity. By the spring of 1959, however, Macmillan had decided his electoral timetable. There would be no vote until after August. The government needed time to use its summit policy to full political advantage.[33] The summit, he told party MPs, was not to be 'a single act [but ...] the beginning of a period of negotiation'.[34] If the heads of government could make some progress at a summer summit, they could then fix 'a date for another meeting, say in December, and try and make progress on something else'.[35] Macmillan's programme was clear: foreign ministers meeting in May, first summit meeting in August, and a general election in October.

The resignation of Dulles in April 1959 seemed to help Macmillan's efforts towards this end. When Dean Rusk became John Kennedy's secretary of state in 1961, he told JFK that his resignation was always on the president's desk. With Dulles, this had been literally true since late 1958 and, on 15 April 1959, Eisenhower reluctantly agreed to release him from the burdens of office. Within six weeks, John Foster Dulles was dead: an era of American foreign policy-making ended. Dulles's replacement was his deputy, Christian Herter, who lacked his boss's breadth of knowledge and international prestige. Most saw Herter, who had severe health problems of his own, as a politician rather than a statesman.[36] His presence served to reinforce Macmillan's argument that this was a meeting of the Second XI, a prelude to the real game.

*

The Geneva foreign ministers conference was a dull affair that achieved very little.[37] Early discussions broke down because of kindergarten-style squabbles about the shape of the table. The Americans wanted a square table, the Soviets demanded it be rectangular, although both finally agreed to Lloyd's exquisite compromise of a lozenge-shaped table. 'Thank goodness one momentous question has been settled without bombs going off,' scathingly observed the *Daily Mail*.[38]

The most important proposal at the Geneva conference was the so-called 'Herter Plan', which suggested four basic stages for solving the German question.[39] First, the Berlin problem had to be considered within the framework of an all-German settlement. East and West Berlin were to be combined through popular election. The rights of the occupying forces would remain. Second, the plan delineated the manner in which the all-German committee on reunification would operate. Third, it proposed a popular vote on the committee's decisions about reunification. Fourth, a peace treaty was to be signed by a newly united Germany and the occupying powers. As far as the US was concerned, Herter had told the national security council that the objective of this proposal was 'to avoid a freezing of the *status quo* in Eastern Europe as a whole which we believe is what the Soviets are most anxious to obtain'.[40] The problem, Selwyn Lloyd had warned cabinet, was that:

> Agreement had been reached on the initial position to be taken up by the Western Powers at the outset of the Geneva meeting. […] It was not to be expected that this initial position would be accepted by the Soviet government; but no attempt had yet been made to identify the concessions which the Western powers might be willing to make in order to reach an agreed settlement.[41]

The Soviets appeared to be equally inflexible.[42] The French foreign minister, Couvé de Murville, wearily concluded after early meetings with Gromyko that 'the Western powers and the Soviets seemed to be talking about two different things. Both sides knew that the other side could not accept its proposals'.[43]

The British press was contemptuous of the foreign ministers proceedings. 'Does anyone know what is going on in Geneva?' inquired the *Daily Herald*. 'We tell you frankly,' it continued, 'we don't and we're prepared to bet that Selwyn Lloyd and Co. don't either.' The time had come when there 'obviously *must* be a summit'.[44] The *Evening Standard* urged that 'the time has come for the extras to leave the stage and for the principals to come on'.[45] Macmillan concurred, but Eisenhower's insistence that 'a summit meeting based on nothing more than wishful thinking would be a disaster' was a disappointment.[46] In the middle of June, he wrote to the president to demand immediate action:

> The heads of government should meet to consider the situation arising from the deadlock in the foreign ministers meeting. What I have in mind, is not that we have the formal summit which has been envisaged [...] but that the Heads of the four governments should meet informally [...] to talk over the situation and try to find a way through the difficulties. If we want an agreement – and surely we do – this is the way to do business with Mr. Khrushchev.[47]

Eisenhower was shocked. Breaking the rules of usual diplomatic practice, he summoned the British ambassador to the White House to give him a humiliating dressing-down. What was the prime minister thinking of, he demanded. Foreign ministers were not schoolboys. Did Macmillan really believe that the president could go 'hat-in-hand to see the Russians at a summit, almost in an attitude of supplication?' That 'did not appeal to the American people [...] and certainly not to me'.[48]

Having vented his anger on Caccia, the president sat down to pen an immediate reply to the prime minister. He knew that Macmillan had 'some particular difficulties' with public opinion. That did not change the fact that an informal summit would be 'interpreted here as a dangerous exhibition of weakness, as indeed I would interpret it'. He continued angrily:

> Frankly, it seems to me that any encounter of the three Western heads of government with Khrushchev would, in fact, be a summit meeting. I think the public would see no difference between an informal and a more formal gathering and I can't see what advantage there would be in the 'informal' formula.[49]

Adding public insult to private injury, Eisenhower told astonished journalists at his daily press call that he deplored British proposals for a summit without progress. It was only in dictatorships that decisions were made 'like Alexander and Napoleon meeting on a raft in a river and settling the fate of the world'.

This was a disingenuous comment given that only the day before he had told aides that he intended to 'ask Mr K. over here to see [me] alone'.[50] On 15 June, Eisenhower approved a note to the Soviet premier.[51] Macmillan did not see the letter until seven days later.[52] Its content was unremarkable. The president expressed his hope that the heads of government would meet soon. He urged the Soviet Premier to seek progress in Geneva. The letter was a 'private and personal note' to which Eisenhower promised he would give 'no publicity whatsoever unless you should desire otherwise'.[53] The day after agreeing the text of this private note to Khrushchev, the president told officials that it was time to 'ask Mr K. over here to see [him], alone'. A Western summit might precede this visit.[54] Eisenhower was taking another step towards an era (perhaps inevitable) of bilateral superpower summitry.

*

The Geneva conference recessed on 20 June, with East and West deadlocked over Berlin. After such an arduous time in Geneva, Lloyd came back to London tired and dispirited. The likely follow-on situation did not look encouraging: more of the same for another few weeks at Geneva, followed either by a break (signalling the end of talks) or by a summons from Khrushchev to a summit. Both situations were potentially embarrassing for the government. If the West rejected Khrushchev's call to the summit, public opinion might feel Khrushchev was morally justified in signing a peace treaty with East Germany. If he went ahead with signing the peace treaty without a call to the summit, the government would be humiliated and, because it would not go to war over this issue, shown up to be impotent. Either way, it would not help at the polls.[55]

This all seemed so obvious to Lloyd and Macmillan. Nevertheless, they were 'at a loss as to how to make the Americans understand'. With Eisenhower, de Gaulle and Adenauer so implacably opposed to a summit without Soviet concessions, the situation was grim. It was imperative that something be done, they agreed, '(a) to avoid risk of a serious catastrophe, perhaps leading … to war, (b) to avoid a grave diplomatic defeat, with corresponding injury to … the Free World, (c) to satisfy British public opinion'.[56] Thus, as Lloyd told cabinet colleagues, 'our task [is …] to persuade the Americans that there were advantages to be gained by holding a meeting of heads of government later in the summer'.[57]

Macmillan had decided to 'bring the president up against the summit issue within the next ten days'.[58] Writing to Eisenhower at the end of June, he urged the president to find a temporary solution for Berlin that might offer a 'prolonged pause' in negotiations and tension. Without actually mentioning a summit meeting, he made it clear that Britain would not go to war without a meeting of the heads of government. The politeness of the language barely concealed the implication that Britain would make a unilateral stand on this issue:

> It would not be easy to persuade the British people that it was in their duty to go to war in defence of West Berlin. After all, in my lifetime we have been dealt two nearly mortal blows by the Germans. People in this country will think it paradoxical, to use a mild term, to have to prepare for an even more horrible war in order to defend the liberties of people who have tried to destroy us twice in this century. […] We and our allies should do and should be seen to do what ordinary people would think reasonable.[59]

Macmillan made clear his real intentions to ambassador Caccia:

> The Americans must realise that if the Geneva talks on
> Berlin produce no result and Gromyko then raises the
> question of a summit, we the British are bound to say that
> we are willing to go to a summit meeting and the onus of
> turning it down will rest with the president and to a lesser
> extent de Gaulle. I have repeatedly told the foreign
> ministers at Geneva that would be our position.[60]

To reinforce the point, Lloyd told the ambassador 'the PM feels
that this is one of the most critical moments in his life and is
determined to press this matter to an issue one way or another in
the next ten days'.[61] Caccia was horrified. Only ten days earlier,
he had been humiliated by Eisenhower in the wake of Macmillan's
earlier letter. Now it seemed that once again he would have to
suffer the president's wrath.

Harold Caccia had taken over as ambassador during the Suez
crisis. In painstaking fashion, he had succeeded in re-establishing
close relations with the White House after that crisis. His efforts
in Washington had made him favourite to succeed Hoyer Millar
as permanent secretary at the foreign office. He had a stake in
maintaining cordial relations with the White House. Therefore,
with Macmillan steeling himself for a fight, Caccia smoothly
urged caution. The whole situation had to be 'exasperating' for
everyone in London, he opined, but surely there was nothing to
be gained from 'pushing the American government machine
faster than it will go'?[62]

Ambassador Reilly in Moscow shared Caccia's concerns.
'Everything suggests that he [Khrushchev] believes the West can
be squeezed out of Berlin', Reilly advised. If the Soviet leader
succeeded in dragging the West to a summit without having
made concessions, 'he would, I think, be encouraged to be
equally unyielding when he gets there'. To achieve anything on
Berlin, the West had to maintain a united front to dispel
Khrushchev's 'hopes on differences between Western allies'.[63]

Demands not to 'rock the boat' now came from all angles. Adenauer publicly complained that 'the difficulty is that America and France have approximately the same point of view, but Great Britain has another. This is already a triumph for Khrushchev'.[64] Eisenhower expressed 'great concern' about the 'wavering qualities of the British on the Berlin and German problems'.[65]

Lloyd knew that Macmillan saw this as perhaps the most critical moment of his career yet advised 'that nothing should be done at this juncture to create an impression … [of] crisis in our discussions'.[66] Macmillan had earlier suggested to the president that they 'meet and talk', an idea which Eisenhower rejected immediately.[67] Denied an opportunity to talk directly to the president, Macmillan constructed for Eisenhower a bizarre agonistic dialogue between 'two citizens' who argued for and against the summit. 'Second Citizen' represented Macmillan's view:

> What I really do want to impress upon you is my fear that … Mr K. may make us all look very foolish and even get us into a dangerous position where we shall not have the moral support of the World. You can't have a first class row without at least trying a summit.[68]

These views of Second Citizen were what 'I might say to the president if I were talking to him'. Astounded by its fourth-rate philosophising, Caccia urged the prime minister not to send the dialogue. The president was a serious and practical man, he reminded him, but not known for his meditative insight. Macmillan concurred. Caccia had narrowly prevented him making a fool of himself.[69]

Macmillan's morale gradually ebbed away in the face of such consistent criticism. He reluctantly accepted the advice of Caccia to let Herter work on the president, but resolved that 'if he loses I shall have to weigh in myself'.[70] Signals from Washington continued to look discouraging. Eisenhower wrote to Macmillan on 27 June to report his comment to the Canadian prime minister that 'the location and the time [of a summit] made very little difference to me'.[71] When time mattered so much to Macmillan, he could only feel frustration at the president's apathy. On 29 June, he fired off another letter to Eisenhower, which shrilly urged him to increase the tempo. 'I am naturally very worried because time is so short and I feel that the decisions we have to take are very grave', he wrote. 'History will never forgive us if we do it wrong. And as you know, it all rests on you and me. This is the burden we must carry'.[72]

The mask of unflappability was slipping as the pretensions to grandeur increased. What Macmillan had failed to detect was that the president's apparent indifference towards an early summit masked plans for a bilateral initiative to Khrushchev. Eisenhower increasingly saw a solution to the current problem as lying not so much with 'you and me' as just 'me'. Herter hit the nail on the head when he predicted that the 'outcome of the Geneva talks will not be a summit, but a talk between the president and Khrushchev'.[73]

*

If June 1959 had been an uncomfortable month for Macmillan, July was worse. Early that month, Herter convinced Lloyd and Caccia that he could effectively represent British interests on the summit question. He discouraged them from taking any unilateral action that might antagonise other allies and back the president into a corner. At the beginning of the month, Macmillan's private secretary, Philip de Zulueta, was talking to the prime minister about 'our understanding with the Americans'. Lloyd instructed Caccia to 'please let Mr Herter know that the prime minister and I are very glad to see that his thoughts are so similar to ours'.[74]

The record of a clandestine conversation on 13 July in Geneva reveals the full extent of what Herter told Lloyd. Herter explained to the foreign secretary that he was about to tell him 'the president's most intimate thoughts' about the summit, information known to only three people in the US. The president, Herter told Lloyd, conceded Macmillan's argument about war being inconceivable without a meeting. Eisenhower believed that a summit was 'inevitable' but thought it would be disastrous coming after failure at Geneva. He had instructed Herter to make a full effort to ensure success at the foreign ministers meeting by putting an interim agreement over Berlin. The heads of government could fill in the blanks. What would happen, Lloyd innocently inquired, if they could not even agree on this? In that case, Herter replied, there would be no reason why the heads of government might not receive alternative proposals.[75]

So here was the president's plan, Herter concluded: a summit meeting in Quebec during the first week of September; the president would invite Khrushchev to Washington before the summit, and Eisenhower would offer to pay a return visit. A Western summit would precede the East-West summit. (But what if de Gaulle refused to come, inquired Lloyd? 'We would just have to have the meeting without him!' replied Herter.) 'The president was very aware of our [the British] timetable and anxious to do anything he could to fit in with that,' concluded Herter.[76]

Macmillan received news of the conversation with 'relief and delight'. Amazed that the president should have had such a 'staggering change of plan', he was delighted that the two friends were again thinking along similar lines.[77] Perplexed by all the manoeuvring at Geneva, he hoped that Herter would 'get on with things'. He told Lloyd that 'I always feel that there is a psychological point in negotiations when one should clinch matters and that if one misses it, agreement becomes impossible. I think that the psychological moment is not far off at Geneva.'[78]

While Macmillan fretted, Eisenhower despatched a letter that formally invited Khrushchev to the United States. Doubt shrouds what happened next. Eisenhower, in his memoirs, claimed that the invitation linked Khrushchev's visit to the US with progress at the Geneva foreign ministers meeting. Neither Under-secretary of State Douglas Dillon nor Under-secretary of State Robert Murphy had believed this to be the case, so much so that when Murphy spoke to Koslov, he made the invitation unqualified. Eisenhower later commented:

> After a bit of cool reflection, I realised the cause of the difficulty lay more in my own failure to make myself unmistakably clear than in the failure of others to understand me. After all, here were some of the most capable men I knew in their field, and apparently all had failed to comprehend the idea in my mind.[79]

The president's disclaimer is disingenuous when seen in the context of American behaviour in Geneva. Herter had told Lloyd that the president would regard *any* progress as sufficient for a summit, but implied that Eisenhower intended to keep his pledge about only going to such a summit after advancement at foreign ministers level. Finally, after months of stalemate, a small measure of progress came in mid-July when Gromyko formally told Herter that the Soviet Union would respect the *status quo* in Berlin at the end of an interim agreement. 'Speaking as the foreign minister of the USSR to the secretary of state of the US', he gravely told Herter, 'the situation [in Berlin] would be exactly the same as today'.[80]

Eisenhower had so frequently demanded this progress. It was not a major advance, but it did represent a step forward. If Herter had correctly reported the president's views to Lloyd on 13 July, Gromyko's pledge on Berlin should have been enough to kick-start the summit process. Certainly Macmillan thought so.

Receiving word from Lloyd about Gromyko's commitment on Berlin, Macmillan began drafting a letter urging the president as 'leader of the western world' to call a summit meeting. The

West could not 'afford to allow things to drag on much longer'. If the West did not accept this small sign of progress, Khrushchev would either sign a treaty with the DDR or himself call for a summit. 'August will not pass without one or the other of these happening', warned Macmillan. If Eisenhower would not demand a meeting, Macmillan threatened, 'it might not always be easy to maintain the solidarity of the western position'.[81]

In his diary, Macmillan wearily conceded that it had been 'a very tiring week – one difficult subject after another. [...] Geneva, the President and Mr K!'[82] He privately admitted to Lloyd:

> If we had the power I would call now for a summit myself, but we must accept that only the Americans have the authority to do this: they are the leaders of the Western world. It follows, therefore, that they must exercise their authority.[83]

Another telegram from Eisenhower dashed Macmillan's hopes. 'What the president says is very bad', Macmillan told Lloyd.[84] 'You are much more hopeful than I am of any worthwhile result at Geneva,' wrote Eisenhower. He added that in his opinion 'the accomplishments will be zero, or even a minus':

> It is still my conviction that such a meeting would be a fraud on our peoples and a great diplomatic blunder. I know there has been some argument that the less the progress at the foreign ministers level, the more necessary a summit meeting becomes. I am quite clear in my mind that such a feeling is not shared by the bulk of our people. This may sound to you overly pessimistic. But you know that I have very much wanted to participate in a meeting in which there was even the slightest promise of a successful outcome. No one would be more thankful than I if my

evaluation of the final Geneva outcome should be demonstrated wrong. But I am trying to be realistic based on what
we know of Khrushchev and his henchmen.[85]

Macmillan was appalled. 'I am getting more and more worried
about the foreign situation', he noted in his diary. 'If we are not
careful, we shall drift into war [with ...] a half-crazy Adenauer,
a cynical and remote de Gaulle, and an amiable but weak
president.'[86] Not only was Eisenhower's message 'very bad', but
it went against the spirit of Lloyd's conversation with Herter.
Suspicious of the secretary's manoeuvring, Macmillan resolved to
confront the president with the 'understanding which I thought
we had reached' with Herter.[87] His anger barely controlled, he
instructed Lloyd to tell Herter:

> I am taking this matter very seriously and am quite deter-
> mined to take action. I am not prepared to put the future of
> my country in jeopardy without a summit. Consequently, I
> am determined next week, if necessary to go and see the
> president or at least to make some public statement of our
> position on the lines of our private communication.[88]

Macmillan had every cause to be wary of Herter's sophistry, but
when Lloyd received the prime minister's telegram, he immediately contacted the foreign office. Macmillan must be told that
there was 'no cause for crisis' and were 'good reasons for not
acting too rapidly'. An emergency telegram that would reveal
everything to the prime minister was on its way.[89]

Lloyd's emergency telegram reported a meeting with Herter
at which they discussed the summit. The meeting had come after
Lloyd sent him a personal letter expressing unequivocal support
for an immediate summit and suggesting it might be 'rather
good' if they could be more 'optimistic' about its prospects. He
was concerned that 'as the hand is being played at the moment,

a position seems to be being built up which, if the president decides to have a summit meeting, it will be represented as a retreat by the West in the face of threatening action and speeches from Khrushchev and the other Russians'.[90]

Lloyd told Herter that he had never 'believed much in the theory of extracting a price for the summit'. He knew that 'the time has come when we should stop thinking that we are going to get any more concessions out of the Soviet Union by being pessimistic about the prospect of a summit meeting taking place'. They had reached a 'critical point' in their negotiations. Now it was better to say there were 'prospects for a summit meeting taking place'. 'After what we have done together to try to keep up a common position,' he concluded threateningly, 'I dread the possibility of our having to take up different positions in public.'[91]

Faced with Lloyd's concerns, Herter was as emollient and charming as ever. He was 'conscious' of Lloyd's fears, which might be allayed by important news: Khrushchev had accepted the president's invitation to visit the United States. Eisenhower was 'sticking to his idea of a summit in Quebec on 1 September, with Mr Khrushchev coming to Camp David for a couple of days beforehand and a meeting of the Western heads of government on 20 August'. He casually added that 'we must remember … Mr Khrushchev has not been told about the president's ideas on a summit or on any of these dates.'[92]

Lloyd reminded Herter that Macmillan was determined to make some public statement in the near future, but the Secretary told him that 'things would move very quickly now'. Gromyko's pledge that 'rights' in Berlin would remain in tact after an interim agreement meant that the foreign ministers could 'recommend to the heads of government that a summit was needed'. However, Herter warned Macmillan not to write to Eisenhower. The president was very 'steamed up' about the whole business. Macmillan's letter might have the 'contrary effect to what was desired'.[93]

'It's very difficult for me', wrote Lloyd to Macmillan, 'in the middle of this conjuring trick out here to know whether all the balls are suddenly going to fall on the ground.' In fact, those balls had already fallen. On 24 July, Lloyd listened in astonishment as the secretary of state revealed that Khrushchev's reply had ignored the link between his visit and progress at Geneva. The problem, Herter explained, was that it would be embarrassing to insist on a link now that the Soviets had accepted the invitation. The president, however, would continue to insist on such a connection. Having disengaged Khrushchev's visit from progress at Geneva, Herter delivered the final blow: Gromyko's pledge about rights in Berlin would not constitute enough progress for a summit.[94]

Lloyd was pole-axed. Could Eisenhower invite Macmillan and de Gaulle to come to the US when Khrushchev was there? he blustered: 'this need not be called a summit'. That was not possible, Herter replied. Perhaps the foreign secretary had allowed electoral considerations to cloud his judgement on this matter. The prime minister's desire for an early summit, Lloyd retorted, was 'not due to electoral considerations rather to his feeling that he had a personal contribution to make'. The secretary of state should understand that 'the main thing for the government from the point of view of the election was to appear to be doing their best'.[95]

Macmillan was upset by American duplicity, but remained touchingly reluctant to believe that his old friend Eisenhower had deceived him. He admitted annoyance and anger, but could not believe the Americans had lied.[96] Writing to Lloyd, Macmillan was 'sure of their good faith', only choosing to doubt 'their drive and power to bring matters to a head'.[97] In the privacy of his diary, he could not hide his sense of betrayal. The Americans were guilty of 'stupidity, naiveté and incompetence'. But actual betrayal? Surely this was more a case of a 'foolish and incredibly naive piece of amateur diplomacy'.[98]

Macmillan was plunged into despair by this turn of events. He had reminded Lloyd on 26 July that 'time is passing on and, as you and I know, time is vital to our plan'.[99] Now proposals for a pre-election summit were in shreds. The spectre of personal and party humiliation loomed:

> My own position here will be greatly weakened. Everyone will assume that the two Great Powers – Russia and USA – are going to fix up a deal over our heads and behind our backs. [...] People will ask, 'Why should UK try to stay in the big game? Why should she be a nuclear power? You told us this would give you power and authority in the world. But you and we have been made fools of. This shows that Gaitskell and Crossman and Co. are right. UK had better give up the struggle and accept, as gracefully as possible, the position of a second rate power.[100]

Angry and bitter, Macmillan sat down on 28 July to pen a frank and accusing letter to Eisenhower. The prime minister described the whole sequence of July's events, including the meeting at which Herter said the president accepted as inevitable a September summit. Macmillan had approved the Khrushchev visit because it formed part of the complete summit package. Now he was 'astonished and distressed' by Eisenhower's about-face. 'I do feel that you have changed your position very radically in the last two weeks,' he continued angrily. 'It is not the change of decision which I regret so much as the evidence which the methods of arriving at your new policy give of a lack of trust between us.'[101]

In Geneva, the breach of trust between Lloyd and Herter by late July was threatening to develop into a serious row. Herter sensed that the increasingly 'nervous' foreign secretary was under considerable pressure from an 'agitated and terribly anxious' Macmillan.[102] Determined to salvage something from the Geneva meetings, Lloyd told him that if Geneva ended with everyone shaking fists at each other, Khrushchev's visit would appear 'crazy to public opinion'.[103] He insisted on issuing a statement that looked forward to a winter summit meeting. Herter unhelpfully responded that such a commitment would be a 'great concession to expect the president to make at this juncture'. Finally, Lloyd lost his temper:

> The president by accepting Khrushchev as his guest and by agreeing to go to the Soviet Union had made the real concessions. That he should swallow that beam and yet boggle the mote of a summit meeting just to discuss the international situation was, to me, fantastic. I thought the whole American attitude was crazy and perhaps the time had come for me to stick straws into my own hair'.[104]

A man of even temperament, Lloyd was not given to shows of emotion, but his impotence was hard to bear. He later reflected to Macmillan that such frustration was the price of friendship with a greater power. The problem, he concluded, was that 'the president is an amateur and Herter is new to the job'. Britain needed to persevere and remember that 'our role is guide, philosopher and friend'. This was 'an exasperating and thankless job but, I fear, a necessary job'.[105]

Macmillan could only agree. 'I do feel very bitter about the way the Americans have behaved', he told Lloyd. 'The future of the Western Alliance must now include, as well as the French problem, the future of Anglo-American relations.'[106] In the short-term, the prime minister could only turn his attention to putting a good spin on Khrushchev's visit to the US. With less than three months to go to election day, time was running out for Harold Macmillan and his Conservative government.

Chapter Four

It has gone off rather well

AUGUST–DECEMBER 1959

MACMILLAN'S FAILURE to achieve a summer summit in 1959 left him dejected and physically exhausted. Everything he had worked for had broken into pieces. Hopes for a pre-election summit had been dashed. Eisenhower and Khrushchev were set to meet at what most commentators would surely regard as a bilateral summit. A western summit seemed unlikely. By August, the flaking veneer of British influence in Washington appeared to be peeling away in front of Macmillan's eyes.[1]

On 5 August 1959, the foreign ministers conference in Geneva finally ground to a halt. Seven days later, President Eisenhower announced to the world that Nikita Khrushchev would be making a visit to the United States 'to see a free people'.[2] 'We had now reached the stage that from an electioneering point of view [a summit] would be better as a prospect in the future than a modified success or even failure in the past', Macmillan reflected in his memoirs. Eisenhower had proposed calling a Western summit to take place before his meeting with Khrushchev, but he had agreed with de Gaulle who 'characteristically – and wisely – would not consider any such idea until Khrushchev's American trip was safely over'.[3]

Macmillan's relaxed after-thoughts do not reflect his thinking at the time. He may have deemed it 'wise' to reject a Western summit when writing in 1972, but thought rather differently in 1959. During those frustrating days, Macmillan encouraged Selwyn Lloyd to support Herter's efforts to push the French into a Western summit meeting. When this failed, Lloyd made a forlorn attempt to convince the American that it would be 'utterly incomprehensible to British opinion' if the president and Khrushchev should arrange return visits 'yet say the time was not ripe for a summit meeting'.[4]

'If you were an ambassador I would say "you spoke well"', Macmillan told the foreign secretary when it was clear that his efforts were to no avail. 'The president has, of course, inadvertently sabotaged the conference, but even before this the Germans and the French made your task very difficult', he continued. 'Looking at it from a distance, I get the impression that Herter, although honourable and friendly, has not much force.'[5] Lloyd was grateful for 'your sympathetic understanding of the difficulties and your expressions of encouragements and confidence'. For all that, he felt an 'intense disappointment and frustration that we have not brought off something concrete in the way of an agreement'.[6]

Amidst so much gloom, it was a great relief when anticipated hostile press commentary did not happen. Indeed, as Macmillan noted:

> No one here has suggested that the Eisenhower-Khrushchev visits are 'negotiating with Russia behind our backs' or a 'sinister deal between the two Great Powers at the expense of smaller powers'. On the contrary, in the UK, as indeed throughout the whole world, this is said to be the result of the Macmillan initiative earlier this year. The British broke the ice. [...] I am relieved that this is the interpretation of history which is universally accepted.[7]

'Cheers! Now they're talking!' proclaimed the banner headline of the *Daily Herald*. 'They say the age of miracles is over,' said the *Daily Mail*, 'but Khrushchev riding down Fifth Avenue ... will seem like a miracle after all that has passed. It is certainly the most wonderful news of its kind for many a long day.' The paper reported Macmillan as being 'delighted' by the news. 'Why should he not be?' it continued, firing an obvious election salvo: 'This is what he had been working for. [...] Britain and the world have good cause to think back with gratitude to the famous white hat – and the man underneath.' Only the centre-left *Observer* hinted at Macmillan's true fears: 'the news of this super-summit between the heads of the two most powerful govern-ments in the world was accepted everywhere ... as the opening of a new era'. Even *The Observer* conceded that 'nearly every-where it appeared to be a popular decision with the man in the street who saw the clouds of war being rolled back. [...] In general, Britain welcomed the move because it was felt to be in the direction pioneered by Mr Macmillan.'[8]

Delight followed when the Americans announced that Eisenhower would undertake a brief European tour before Khrushchev's visit to the US.[9] The president felt that the Allies needed some reassurance. Perhaps more significantly he wanted the chance to try out his new presidential jet plane Air Force One.[10] When he set off for Europe on 26 August, the president felt at the peak of his powers speeding above the Atlantic. His personal secretary, Ann Whitman, affectionately noted in her diary that 'the newspaper people suddenly find they have been wrong in riding the president, that he is not an 'old and sick and feeble' man, with no powers because of the fact that he cannot run again. They have discovered that his popularity is higher than ever, that the people of the country would solidly re-elect him tomorrow.[11]

Whatever the state of public opinion in America, Eisenhower might have been excused for thinking that the people of Europe would have voted for him to lead them. The former Supreme Allied Commander received a rapturous, emotional welcome everywhere. Whatever differences existed within the Western Alliance, Eisenhower remained to ordinary people the general who had won the second world war.

Paris gave Eisenhower a hero's reception. 'How many?' he asked as he rode in slow procession through the streets with de Gaulle. 'At least a million', the French president replied. 'I did not expect half so many,' said Eisenhower, clearly moved.[12] His visit came days after the fifteenth anniversary of the liberation of Paris. It was a pertinent reminder to a troublesome ally that France owed its liberty to Eisenhower and the Americans. The reception in Paris suggested that the French needed no reminding.

From Paris via Bonn, where he was 'astonished' by the exuberant crowds, Eisenhower flew to Britain. He 'felt as if I were coming home' on arriving in London. 'Well, here I am again,' he exclaimed to Macmillan on the tarmac at Heathrow.[13]

It could not have been a more joyous 'homecoming'. The car bearing the president and Macmillan crept along at a walking place for its seventeen-mile journey from London Airport. The crowds cheered and waved, many in tears, hailing a returning hero. 'I never would have believed it,' Macmillan kept telling the president.[14] As the *Evening Standard* commented, the British people were welcoming Eisenhower as 'an old friend, [...] with affection as a man with whom they shared the experience of danger and the exhilaration of victory'.[15]

When the two leaders sat down at Chequers for their only official talk during the visit, Eisenhower expressed his hope that Khrushchev might appear more 'generous' than usual in America by agreeing to an interim arrangement about Berlin. To avoid any suggestion of a bilateral negotiation, Eisenhower would not make any announcement about possible achievements until Khrushchev was on his way home. He reiterated, however, that there could be no summit without Soviet concessions. On Berlin, the president said an interim agreement might lead to complete troop withdrawal in advance of German re-unification.

He had told Adenauer not to be so negative about everything, noting that the Americans were 'getting tired of having always to say "no" to every new suggestion'.[16]

Eisenhower had not come to Britain to negotiate. He was there to enjoy a nostalgic 'trip down memory lane' whilst helping an old friend in an election. The president hosted a dinner at the US embassy for his wartime comrades, at which Macmillan thoughtfully ranked himself as Political Adviser (AFHQ) thus allowing Eisenhower to sit between old comrades Lords Alanbrooke and Alexander. He flew to Balmoral for two days, where the Queen surprised everyone by meeting him at the gates to walk arm-in-arm up to the house. Eisenhower also spent a few days holidaying in Culzean Castle – a present from the people of Scotland in thanks for his wartime endeavours. Even at Chequers, only a couple of hours had been used for 'business'; the rest of the time was spent hitting golf balls and reminiscing.[17]

The visit was one of the happiest times of Eisenhower's presidency. With uncharacteristic emotion, he wrote to Macmillan during the trip that 'the welcome given to me by you – and by so many wonderful people of this island – has warmed and touched my heart beyond any words at my command'. Later he added:

> The unique and friendly character of this latest of our conferences [...] was engendered not so much by the warm welcome of the English people – heart-warming as it was – but by the close relationship between the two of us that seemingly grows stronger every time we meet.[18]

Macmillan himself was delighted with the trip. Writing to Eisenhower, he enthused:

> In a way this was a tribute to you as president of the United States, our great ally and friend and the firm rock of the Alliance; yet, it was a real personal triumph for you. I rejoice at it with all my heart.[19]

This was a genuine expression. Yet Macmillan did not rejoice simply because the trip was a personal triumph for the president. It was also a reflected triumph for himself.

Macmillan had seized the opportunity to use Eisenhower's visit for the opening shots in the (unofficial) general election campaign. John Foster Dulles had commented earlier that 'we are not unsympathetic to this since we don't want to see [Nye] Bevan win the election'.[20] Thus, friendship and national interest happily overlapped for Eisenhower. This was not the first time his administration had aided the Conservative party. Lloyd had already recalled the Americans being 'very helpful' in 1955, and hoped they might 'take a similar position of helpfulness at this time'.[21]

The Eisenhower visit was a stunning public relations success. Macmillan brilliantly affected the role of international statesman riding high above sordid national politics. He travelled in the car with the president as the crowds cheered. Everywhere they went, it was as two old friends laughing and chatting, each clearly enjoying the other's company. After the final dinner of the visit at 10 Downing Street, Eisenhower went on an unscheduled 'walkabout' during which he strolled with his arm around Macmillan's shoulder. It could not have appeared more chummy, as the morning editions showed.[22]

Macmillan was already adept at finding media opportunities. He had taken advice in the art of television from the comedian Bud Flanagan. He made a point of being available on a regular basis for interviews. He knew how to draw attention to himself (such as with his Moscow white fur hat).[23] However, it was during the president's visit that he pulled off the finest television coup of his career. He persuaded Eisenhower to appear with him in a live TV discussion from the state drawing room at 10 Downing Street. In what amounted to a Conservative party political broadcast, prime minister and president enjoyed a cosy chat to express total confidence in one another. Indeed, Eisenhower's only concern seemed to be that, with No. 10

undergoing repair, the two leaders might fall through the floor. When their conversation ended, the two old friends were seen sauntering off to an adjoining room where assembled guests, including Churchill, broke into 'spontaneous' applause. 'The first account from viewers seems to be very enthusiastic', Macmillan cheerfully recorded afterwards.[24]

The press too were impressed. The *Daily Mail* described the broadcast as a 'virtuoso display by a polished television performer'. They praised the prime minister as smooth and suave, totally in control of the situation, a view shared by the *Evening Standard*. *The Observer* complained that Macmillan had gone 'dangerously near the edge of political taste', adding piously that 'we are meant to be choosing between parties not detergents'. Yet even the hostile *Daily Herald* endorsed Macmillan's projection of his relationship with the president. 'Being in public, the two leaders addressed each other formally as Mr President and Mr Prime Minister,' it noted. 'But, just once, Ike slipped and said "Harold". Maybe this was the most revealing moment of the whole performance.'[25]

The broadcast was a stunning electoral coup for Macmillan. Labour's Herbert Morrison conceded that the 'slight, if understandable, exaggeration which gave the public the idea that the two men enjoyed a long, intimate association [...] offered wonderful election propaganda on the eve of the polling date'.[26] Brendan Bruce, who was Margaret Thatcher's director of communications at Conservative central office during the 1980s, comments of this seminal television broadcast:

> The image of a national leader above party politics and on first name terms with the most powerful, popular and respected leader in the West was extremely effective. Macmillan had understood one simple and vitally important fact about the new medium: *how* you look is as (sometimes more) important as *what* you say.[27]

*

Returning to Washington after a triumphant European tour, Eisenhower felt ready to face the challenge presented by the Khrushchev visit. He told senior members of Congress that he was determined to 'make this great personal effort before leaving office to see if it might not be useful in softening up the Russian leader even just a little bit'.[28] The president's reasoning was touchingly simple: 'K. has never seen a great people living in freedom. [...] He should have the sight of people as they work and live as they please. He is possessed of a terrible power – we must make sure he is not mistaken about America'. Like Macmillan before him, Eisenhower wanted to make a personal impact on the Soviet Chairman. Crucial private talks would take place at the president's Camp David retreat. There Eisenhower would seek to convince Khrushchev that the latter had the opportunity 'to be the greatest man of our time – instead of offering a closed fist to the peoples, if he would just give a little, he can finally go down in history as a great man'.[29]

Khrushchev arrived at Andrews Air force Base just after noon on 15 September. Khrushchev, like Eisenhower, enjoyed travel for its own sake and coupled this with an insatiable curiosity about other countries. He had a natural suspicion of advice from officials, a trait forged in the paranoid times of High Stalinism. He felt the best way to judge a situation was to go and look. He had supreme confidence in his own debating skill and would frequently attempt to intimidate other leaders. If he detected signs of weakness he would, in the words of John Kennedy (who was bullied by Khrushchev at Vienna in 1961) 'just beat the hell out' of them.[30] At the first official meeting at the White House, Khrushchev amusingly gave the president a model of a Soviet moon-shot rocket.[31] A slightly bemused Eisenhower was unsure as to whether this was a jibe about the Soviet lead in the space race, or a 'completely sincere' gesture.[32] Khrushchev took a helicopter ride over Washington DC but, much to the president's disappointment, was unimpressed by all the middle-class houses and rush-hour motor cars down below.[33] After an initial few days in the capital, Khrushchev set off on a whistle-stop tour of the States. It was a huge media success, involving bemusement about Disneyland, astonishment at Hollywood showgirls, and an outrageous speech at the UN calling for total disarmament in four years with no inspection or supervision. Khrushchev had always recognised that ideas, psychology and propaganda were as important as bombs in winning the cold war.[34]

After the tour came two days of talks at Camp David. Eisenhower wanted to get the chairman on his own, away from the 'evil and stupid' Menshikov, who had been 'feeding poison' to him throughout the trip.[35] Their meetings were convivial. The two leaders spent time together walking and chatting. Eisenhower even drove the premier to his Gettysburg farm to meet his grandchildren. Gromyko recalled that at all times Eisenhower 'tried to create a pleasant atmosphere and in general behaved as though he wanted constructive relations'.[36]

Conversations were calm and dispassionate. There were no outbursts from Khrushchev as there had been with Macmillan. Discussion centred on the question of Berlin. 'United States people believed that they are in shadow of some threat of unilateral action in Berlin', Eisenhower explained. He had to know that the president 'would have to resign before he could accept any time limit for the United States withdrawal from Berlin'.[37] Khrushchev responded that the Soviet Union 'could accept no agreement which implied the indefinite perpetuation of the "occupation regime" in Berlin', and that it was 'an impossible condition to demand that no Western rights in Berlin be affected'.[38] Thus, the leaders of the two superpowers came up against the issue that had deadlocked the foreign ministers talks in Geneva. The record is unclear about this discussion, but they seemed to make some kind of 'gentlemen's agreement' about Berlin.[39] Henry Cabot Lodge concluded that Khrushchev and Eisenhower had simply decided to 'keep talking'.[40]

On his return to Moscow, Khrushchev addressed seventeen thousand of the Party faithful who had packed into the Lenin Sports Palace to welcome him home. There he passionately declared:

> I must say from this high platform to the Muscovites and to all our people, the government and the party, that President Dwight Eisenhower has displayed wise statesmanship in assessing the present international situation. He has shown courage and valour (stormy applause) [...] We could not, of course, clear out with the president at one go all the cold war rubble that has piled up during the years … But I will tell you frankly dear Comrades that I got the impression that the president sincerely wanted to liquidate the cold war and improve relations between our two countries. (stormy applause)[41]

Eisenhower was delighted. Khrushchev was honouring their 'gentlemen's agreement'. In turn, the president confirmed to the world's press that his conversations with the Soviet leader had removed his objections to a summit. Slightly lamely, he noted that 'there is progress because we are not at an impasse'. Naturally, he would consult allies. But at last, it seemed that the summit was on.[42]

*

Watching anxiously from London, Macmillan thought it 'curious' that although the president 'has said he is consulting his allies on these matters, we have received no real approach from him'.[43] Indeed, when Eisenhower wrote to the prime minister after the visit, he did not refer at all to the substance of his talks with Khrushchev or a prospective summit. Eisenhower had announced progress to the world's press, but the British could not see that anything had changed.

The French were equally bemused. Sir Frederick Hoyer Millar, permanent secretary at the foreign office, consulted the French ambassador, Chauvel, who also confessed that 'it was not at all clear to him exactly what it was that Khrushchev had said about Germany or Berlin that had enabled President Eisenhower to say that sufficient progress had now been made to justify the holding of a summit meeting'. Hoyer Millar admitted that 'we too were equally in the dark'.[44]

Macmillan immediately wrote to Harold Caccia in Washington to complain that he knew less than the media about progress between Eisenhower and Khrushchev. Caccia replied that there was no cause for concern. The president knew Macmillan wanted a summit and 'would probably be ready to go along with this despite the doubts of Mr Herter and Mr Merchant, provided that General de Gaulle and Chancellor Adenauer do not protest too vehemently'. Eisenhower's current reticence on the subject, he concluded, was because the British election was just one week away.[45]

Macmillan was dumbfounded. For almost a year, he had pinned his electoral fortunes on the achievement of a summit. Now, having dropped his objections, the president had turned bashful. On the first day of October, he wrote to Eisenhower to move things along. There were congratulations on 'seizing the initiative' with a 'pretty difficult customer', along with praise for winning 'Khrushchev's agreement to remove the element of the threat from the Berlin situation'. Khrushchev had 'stuck to his word and confirmed this change of position after he got back to Moscow'. With this achieved, Macmillan felt sure the president 'would agree that this advance by the Russians had cleared the way to the summit'.[46]

Macmillan also made a private appeal for an announcement on a summit before the election. Hoyer Millar informed Caccia that the prime minister was 'particularly anxious to try and make some progress during the next few days'. Nevertheless, he

warned that Macmillan's letter to the president would have to be
a matter of utmost secrecy:

> In view of the contents of the penultimate paragraph of the
> message, please try to ensure that the Americans treat it as
> a purely personal communication. [...] You should also take
> suitable steps about handling of the message in the embassy.
> For your own information the text which will be entered in
> the FO files will omit the penultimate paragraph. You may
> wish to do the same at your end. Please burn after perusal.[47]

When Caccia replied, he reassured Hoyer Millar that he had
delivered the prime minister's letter in circumstances that would
ensure 'my visit should not be noticed'. Herter promised the
ambassador that the letter would go into his personal files
without anyone at the state department seeing it.[48] Eisenhower's
reply makes clear exactly what Macmillan had asked of the
president. The summit, Eisenhower wrote, would come from
'diplomatic negotiation leading to a simultaneous announcement
from the four capitals rather than that the initiative should be
taken by myself'.[49]

The president, Herter told Caccia, was 'extremely sorry that
he could not go further', but 'it was not possible to get the Allies
to accept the proposition in time and Khrushchev would also
have to be got to agree'. He also warned him that it would not
'look well if you used words which might be represented as
meaning that some bilateral agreement had been reached
between yourself and the president of the US before others
concerned had been approached let alone squared'.[50]

Macmillan chose to ignore Herter's warning and risk an
American contradiction. He continued to imply that a summit
was just around the corner. The date, he declared, would be
fixed in a 'few days'. This brought a swift denial from the White
House. Senior Labour figures accused Macmillan of 'playing

party politics with the summit'.[51] Nevertheless, he continued to argue right up to the election that this was simply a matter of fixing 'the date and the place'.[52] When a visibly upset German ambassador called at the foreign office to complain about press reports that Macmillan would soon announce a summit, he was bluntly told to 'use his nut … since foreign affairs was a key issue in this election, the PM could not be expected either not to welcome the improved prospects of a summit or to minimise the role which we could play there'.[53]

On the morning of polling day, *The Times* predicted a twenty-two seat majority for the Conservatives. In fact, they achieved a staggering hundred-seat majority.[54] Macmillan had based his campaign strategy on the twin promises of future 'prosperity and peace'.[55] Government financial policy had stimulated a boom in 1959 that seemed to give substance to the feeling that Britain had 'never had it so good'.[56] As to peace, Macmillan had written in the Tory manifesto:

> It is the supreme purpose of all policy. I have lived through two wars and all my efforts are directed to prevent a third. Events of the last few months have given me hope that we may be moving into a more constructive period. Vital international negotiations lie ahead and I ask you to continue to entrust them to a Conservative government.[57]

Macmillan's summitry had successfully neutered criticism of Conservative foreign policy sustained during Suez. Bold initiatives had given a sense of British dynamism and leadership on the world stage.[58] The biggest single step in that restoration of favour had come during the Moscow visit, when Macmillan took a public opinion poll lead for the first time in his premiership. Polls around the election showed that forty-three per cent of voters thought the Conservatives could handle best a summit as opposed to twenty-one per cent for Labour.[59] Only eight per cent of voters now expressed themselves 'especially concerned' about the H-bomb.[60] The *Evening Standard* captured a new feeling in an editorial commemorating the twentieth anniversary of the outbreak of the second world war:

> Nothing is more reassuring than the contrast between 1939 and 1959. Optimism about the future is not based on the naive assumption there are no causes of conflict in the world today; or that these can be easily resolved. It springs from the belief that the disputes can be settled without war. [...] If President Eisenhower and Mr Macmillan persist with their efforts despite the opposition they will encounter, people in September 1979 may be celebrating another anniversary. They may remember not Hitler's war but the beginning of Eisenhower's and Macmillan's drive to make the world a more placid, less jittery place to live.[61]

The peace movement was out of touch with this new positive mood. Although CND had the support of candidates in 286 marginal constituencies, including 211 from Labour, it won only a handful. Several prominent supporters lost their seats. The overall result of the election, extremely disappointing for CND, caused widespread dismay within the peace lobby. A special 'CND week' flopped. The H-bomb attracted little attention during the campaign. The 1959 election served notice that the public had concluded British unilateral nuclear disarmament would have little impact on the cold war.[62]

The election was a personal triumph for Macmillan. The myth of 'Supermac' now had substance. Labour's Herbert Morrison conceded that the Conservative re-election, just three years after the Suez debacle, was 'largely due to the skilful politics of Harold Macmillan, together with his intuitive understanding of a large proportion of the British people'.[63] In public, Macmillan retained his customary finesse. 'It has gone off rather well', he nonchalantly told reporters.[64] In private, he confessed to feeling awed.[65]

*

Electoral expediency drove Macmillan's summit policy. Yet with the election won, his thoughts remained on personal diplomacy. He had proven himself a consummate master of domestic politics. Now he moved his sights to his place in history as a world statesman. Churchill had been the great champion of summits. A profitable summit series might crown Macmillan as Churchill's true heir.[66]

Macmillan resolved to keep his loyal lieutenant, Selwyn Lloyd, at the foreign office at least until the summer. Then he could move sideways. Macmillan knew the foreign secretary was 'tired, not only with the burden of office but by the long and wearisome foreign negotiations in which he had been involved'.[67] Lloyd had come in for harsh press criticism during the election campaign. Massingham of the *Observer* had noted vitriolicly that 'his great asset to the PM is that when he is dropped, no-one will notice his departure'.[68] Lloyd agreed to stay on, but commented ruefully of the media attacks: 'Does all this worry one? Of course it does – perhaps irritate rather than worry is the word'.[69]

On 9 October, the day following the British election, Eisenhower lost his hesitancy concerning a summit. He wrote to Macmillan, de Gaulle and Adenauer outlining the discussions that had taken place at Camp David. He told them that Khrushchev had proposed a summit meeting. He asked for 'your views on how I should reply to this proposal'. He made it clear that in his view 'the Camp David talks removed many of the objections to a summit conference'. Khrushchev had shown a 'sufficient indication of a change of tone to justify further exploration'. 'It would probably be wise to arrange a summit meeting within the reasonable future', he concluded. 'I hope you would agree we should now proceed to do so'.[70]

'Having dragged his feet for so long', Macmillan dryly observed in his memoirs, Ike 'was now in something of a hurry'.[71] Eisenhower suggested that there might be 'some advantage to a summit meeting in December'.[72] He was approaching his last year in office. American domestic politics were at a virtual standstill. Republicans and Democrats were already winding themselves up for the 1960 election. The primaries would begin in early 1960. In the summer, each party convention would choose their new standard-bearers. By that time, Eisenhower would be a 'lame duck' president without the authority to push through Congress ratification of any agreement he might sign with Khrushchev. Eisenhower was as concerned as Macmillan was about his place in history. First he had to contend with French obduracy.[73]

There was certain ambivalence in de Gaulle's attitude towards America. At moments of crisis, he could be a staunch and loyal ally.[74] At other times, he was irritating and pointlessly difficult about matters of apparently little consequence. His reasoning was straightforward: France belonged to the Western Alliance and when the USSR threatened the West, France would show complete solidarity with its own side. When there was no threat, France had to follow an independent line precisely because it was Western. The Alliance tied France to the USA, which was economically and militarily superior. In such a position, de Gaulle reasoned, France simply had to be difficult and independent in order to raise its rank and importance as an ally.[75] In de Gaulle's own words, France was ready 'to demand and to act'.[76]

De Gaulle had welcomed the signing of the Atlantic Pact in 1949, but the Soviet nuclear capability had transformed the situation. Now that the USSR had the weapons and delivery systems to inflict huge damage on the US, it would be logical for the two superpowers to conduct nuclear exchanges away from their own territory. This made Europe the most likely theatre of war. De Gaulle therefore concluded that 'for Western Europeans,

NATO had thus ceased to guarantee their survival. Once the efficacy of the protection had become doubtful, why leave one's destiny in the hands of the protector?'[77]

De Gaulle had outlined the full extent of his plans to Eisenhower during the president's visit to Paris in September 1959. Sitting by the fire in their dressing gowns, the two generals reminisced about the war. When the conversation finally turned to political matters, de Gaulle told Eisenhower of when France would conduct its first nuclear explosion and then explained with great honesty why he wanted France to be an independent nuclear nation:

> You, Eisenhower, would wage nuclear war for Europe, because you know the interests that are at stake. But as the Soviet Union develops its capacity to strike the cities of North America, one of your successors will agree to wage nuclear war only to confront and attack at the same time against this continent. When that time comes, I or my successor will have to possess the necessary means to change into nuclear war what the Soviets would have liked to remain a classic war. [...] The Soviets know me. They know that if I possess the strike force, in order to respond to an invasion of Western Europe, I shall use it, and that will be an extra dissuasion for them. To do that, I have to be unbearable on my own.[78]

'De Gaulle isn't entirely in the wrong with his nuclear programme,' Eisenhower had mused to an aide, 'I'd like to help him in some way or other, but I can't.' The president might have favoured helping France, but debate on the subject was so bitter in Washington that he was able to do no more than offer informal encouragement.[79]

De Gaulle's answer to this situation, as he had bluntly warned Eisenhower, was that 'unbearable'. During the autumn of 1959, he did his best to live up to that promise. He resolved to secure three items on his personal agenda before attending a heads of government summit meeting. First, France must explode an atomic bomb so that he would sit at the conference table as the leader of a nuclear power. Second, his resistance to an early summit might extract favourable positions from Britain and America in UN debates about Algeria. Third, he wanted to meet Khrushchev alone, like Macmillan and Eisenhower, before facing him across the negotiating table. He would not rush into an early summit when his position would be so much stronger by the spring. Consequently, the French president's behaviour towards allies would be insufferable in the remaining months of 1959.[80]

De Gaulle wrote to the prime minister on 20 October to propose a summit conference for the end of May or the beginning of June 1960. He explained:

> Now frankly I do not think that it is in our interest to hasten to the opening of this meeting with Mr Khrushchev which will lead to the confrontation of irreconcilable policies, but at the same time be decisive. It seems to me that we should first of all see how his professed intentions for an international détente develop. The debates in the United Nations, the pattern of events in South East Asia, in the East and in Africa will enable us to see this more clearly. As for Berlin, there is no hurry.[81]

Sir Gladwyn Jebb, British ambassador to Paris, reported to London that foreign minister Couvé de Murville had told of French puzzlement at American haste. They had respected (if not agreed with) Macmillan's demands for an early summit after his Moscow visit, but this sudden about-turn by the Americans could only be explained by Eisenhower having concluded a private deal with Khrushchev at Camp David. De Gaulle believed that America's 'lag' in the missile race drove its summit policy.

The Eisenhower administration felt 'the need for a truce in the cold war even if this were achieved by certain concessions in the political field so that they might be able to catch up'. Jebb concluded 'it is obvious that the General is sticking to his guns; I am afraid my guess is that he will continue to do so'.[82]

At a subsequent meeting with Lloyd, ambassador Chauvel outlined reasons for French opposition to an immediate summit. De Gaulle would not co-operate until the UN had debated the Algerian question, and he, like Macmillan and Eisenhower, had held personal talks with Khrushchev.[83] To these factors, ambassador Jebb added a third: 'it is only too likely that this ... has some relation to the prospective [nuclear] explosion in the Sahara'.[84]

*

If de Gaulle had wished to slow down the summit process, Eisenhower had every reason for wanting it to move faster. Balance of payments difficulties and fears about the 'missile gap' would cause problems for a Republican presidential candidate (particularly if that candidate was vice-president Richard Nixon). Republican campaigners were telling the president that a summit meeting followed by a personal visit to the USSR would sweep the party's candidate into the White House on wave of optimism about a thaw in the cold war.[85]

Eisenhower was also concerned that de Gaulle's timetable might compromise the 'spirit of Camp David' because Khrushchev would interpret it as a stalling mechanism.[86] Eisenhower knew the Russian had taken a considerable political risk by visiting the United States.[87] Voices in the Soviet government had complained that the trip made the leader of World Communism appear like a travelling salesman. Foreign Ministry officials had expressed concern about the effect the policy would have on allies, especially China. On returning to Moscow from America, Khrushchev had claimed a special bond with Eisenhower that promised to lead to detente. He needed a summit 'before the end of year', the Soviet UN envoy, Valerian Zorin, told the White House. The longer the delay, the less room for manoeuvre Khrushchev would have with the opponents of his policy.[88]

The looming presidential elections and fears about losing the spirit of Camp David convinced Eisenhower of the need to act immediately to pull rank on his allies. Perhaps it was time to 'get tough with Britain, Germany and France', he suggested to Herter, adding that 'the United States, after all, paid for most of the air bases and other infrastructure, and has paid the whole cost of atomic weapons'. The time had come when 'we should put no more military assistance into Europe. They are now able to support themselves'.[89] When Herter told Caccia that the president might want to discuss this subject, the ambassador conceded that it would come as 'a pretty big cat among the pigeons'.[90] Faced with recalcitrant allies in Europe who looked set to spoil his last year in office, Eisenhower reflected that it was time to play 'hardball'.[91]

*

De Gaulle's unwillingness to agree to an immediate summit frustrated Macmillan as well as Eisenhower. 'To postpone it for several months will be a grave disappointment to public opinion, will lose all the present impetus and may cause K to go sour', he wrote to Eisenhower.[92] However, when ambassador Caccia reported that the president wanted a Western summit in December, Macmillan resigned himself to waiting until 1960 for a full summit.[93] 'President Eisenhower is disgusted at the delay, but not disposed to argue any more,' Macmillan recorded in his diary. 'So then I have agreed. But we have refused his proposed date – April – for the real summit. What Mr K will now do is obscure. He may well turn nasty and start sending ultimatums again about Berlin. Then – through the folly, first of the

Americans and then of the French, we shall have lost all the ground which I gained by the Moscow visit.'[94]

A month before the Western summit, Macmillan told Australia's prime minister, Robert Menzies, that 'my main preoccupation is still with East-West relations in general and the plans for a summit meeting in particular':

> I believe that a summit meeting would be useful even if it did not result in very concrete agreements, simply because these meetings turn men's minds towards negotiation and discussion and away from war. It seems absurd to me to suppose that we could have a meeting like the congress of Vienna lasting for months and deciding the whole range of issues between East and West. What I envisage is a series of meetings, each one leading on to the next, and making per-haps some modest progress in all these complicated matters. [...] Even if a summit meeting was not to make any progress at all I would feel that it could nevertheless serve a useful purpose provided that it led to a further conference.[95]

Securing American and French agreement to the principle of a summit series was Macmillan's main strategic aim at the Western summit. His immediate problem was convincing de Gaulle to attend a full summit meeting as early as possible. Judged by these criteria, the results of the Western summit were mixed for Macmillan. Conversations were friendly. De Gaulle conducted proceedings with grace and charm. During the first meeting at the Elysée on 19 December, he paid tribute to Macmillan for the Moscow initiative, and accepted his argument that a summit should be held. Only the when and where remained unanswered.[96]

The question of when was determined by de Gaulle. He insisted that he would not attend a summit until he had seen Khrushchev in Paris and the president in Washington. Khrushchev was coming to France on 15 March; de Gaulle was making a Head of State visit to Britain in early April. He hoped to go to Washington in mid-April. Thus he would not attend a summit until the end of April. 'I guess I'll just have to clear my schedule,' grumbled Eisenhower.[97] Macmillan knew that Khrushchev would be unable to accept this date because it clashed with the Soviet May Day celebrations. Thus the summit would not take place until the middle of May, just as de Gaulle had predicted in the summer of 1959.[98]

Macmillan had been desperate for an earlier summit, but with the election won, he was relieved that finally they had arranged a meeting. If he suffered any disappointment over the date, he felt more than compensated by arrangements about the place. It had seemed inevitable that Geneva, traditional place of international negotiations, would once again host the summit meeting. However, to everyone's surprise, de Gaulle intervened on this matter. 'Ce n'est pas gai,' he complained wearily of Geneva. This was 'so General de Gaulle', Macmillan later recalled, but it did give him a wonderful opportunity to suggest Paris as a suitable venue. Having observed de Gaulle over many decades, Macmillan correctly judged that the general's vanity would not allow him to reject such a proposal. With Paris agreed as the venue for the summit, de Gaulle could hardly complain about further meetings held in each of the remaining three capitals. Eisenhower agreed. The principle of a summit series was accepted.[99] Macmillan was delighted. Adenauer would later accuse him of trying to 'organise world government'. In a sense, he was right. Macmillan later admitted in his memoirs:

> Might there not be a hope that little by little if the meetings between East and West ... became part of the accepted instrument by which peace was to be maintained and the progress of mankind ensured we might be embarking upon a practical method of making effective the ideas of the founders of the United Nations organisation? What the

Security Council had failed to do in New York in the atmosphere of intrigue and confusion in that vast assembly might perhaps be gradually brought about in the quiet meetings of four statesmen held in regular sequence in one or other of their capitals.[100]

The western leaders despatched a letter to Khrushchev telling him of their wish 'for the four Heads of State or government to meet together from time to time in each others' countries to discuss the main problems affecting the attainment of peace and stability in the world'. They proposed a first meeting in Paris on 27 April 1960.[101]

When the summit was over Macmillan returned home happily for Christmas. 'A lot of good talks have taken place, and a very good atmosphere of confidence and friendship created,' he recorded in his diary.[102] To Lloyd he gleefully concluded that 'on the summit therefore, particularly on the idea of a series of summits – assuming Mr Khrushchev accepts – we have achieved our objectives'.[103] Lloyd replied that 'your suggestion of Paris for the first meeting gave us the series. We could hardly have expected this aspect to go so well.'[104]

The final piece of the puzzle slipped into to place on Christmas Day when Gromyko handed Khrushchev's reply to the Western ambassadors. This expressed his 'deep satisfaction that you [...] consider it desirable for the discussion of the main international problems from time to time to arrange a meeting at the highest level'. He strongly believed it was 'through the personal meetings of statesmen on the highest level that urgent international problems can be solved in the most effective manner'. Khrushchev also accepted Paris as a venue for the talks. Only the date was inconvenient. He suggested they meet on either 21 April or 4 May 1960.[105] After checking their diaries, the leaders all agreed to meet in Paris on 16 May.[106]

Macmillan had worked for a heads of government conference for a year. Finally, with 1959 at its close, the summit was on, and Macmillan could relax. 'Shoot at Arundel', he recorded happily of the day he received news of the summit. 'A lovely day and a most delightful shoot – about 170 high pheasants.'[107]

Chapter Five

One chance in a million

JANUARY–MAY 1960

HAROLD MACMILLAN HAD spent 1959 worrying about how to bring about an East/West summit meeting. At the outset of 1960, he was able to reflect on a year of unexpected success. His visit to Moscow had been a triumph (eventually), a date for the summit was set (finally), and the election won (convincingly). Not without justification, Macmillan believed that everything was at last working to plan. Yet that plan was part of a much broader strategy to recalibrate British foreign policy to ensure a place on the world stage without straining resources beyond breaking point.

Shortly after becoming prime minister, Macmillan had initiated a far-reaching study of Britain's place in the world. A committee under the chairmanship of Sir Patrick Dean of the Foreign Office reported to a steering committee headed by cabinet secretary Sir Norman Brook. Its task was to set the direction of British future policy until 1970. Macmillan circulated the cabinet with the final product, 'Future Policy, 1960–1970,' on 24 February 1960 for discussion at a series of meetings in March.[1]

The conclusion on Britain's prospects offered by 'Future Policy' was, in the laconic words of Lord Hailsham, 'somewhat disappointing and depressing'.[2] A technical assessment of

Britain's resources attempted to balance defence programmes with other claims on the National Product. It also detailed the overseas' component of public expenditure. It presented a worrying analysis of the frailty of sterling, the disproportionate defence burden that the UK bore in comparison with allies and its crippling impact on British reserves. The report affirmed a long-held Treasury position that 'our own ability to bear the burden of defence-like expenditure depends to a considerable extent upon the size of the burden borne by our NATO (and Commonwealth) partners in relation to their resources'.[3]

Despite a gloomy economic assessment, the report judged that British influence need not shrink in proportion to its relative material strength if other 'intangible assets' were used 'in the right way'. If Britain were to survive as a Great Power, it was imperative to 'avoid an absolute choice between North America on the one hand and the continent of Europe on the other; we should rather aim to bind together one comprehensive Atlantic Community'.[4] The Commonwealth was unimportant: 'the truth is that [it] is not and will never be a source of power in absolute terms comparable with say the USA or possibly Western Europe'. This conclusion, wrote Dean to the foreign secretary, was at 'the heart of the whole report'.[5]

Although the Future Policy Committee made a clear recommendation on avoiding a final choice between America and Europe, the paper urged a new relationship with the Common Market. This coincided with Macmillan's own thoughts on Europe. 'For better or for worse the [Common Market] looks like being here to stay', he had told Selwyn Lloyd in October 1959. The question is how to live with the Common Market economically and turn its political effects into channels harmless to us'.[6]

Lloyd had advised Macmillan in December 1959 that Britain's immediate priority was to 'prevent the Six supplanting us as the principal influence on the United States policy' by trying 'to play in the game both as pro-Europeans and pro-Atlantic Community'.[7] He reminded the prime minister that Britain had been actively considering a closer relationship with continental Europe since 1956, although the 'severe shock' of the Suez crisis had blown this off course. Macmillan, on becoming prime minister, had been able to take advantage of his 'old personal relationship with the [US] president' to repair the damage caused by Suez. This inevitably ensured that British policy 'switched back from Europe and turned towards the United States'. That policy had 'brought solid advantages to us'.[8] Nevertheless, Lloyd foresaw 'difficulties' that would 'increase with the next United States administration'. Washington increasingly saw the French and Germans as solid and tough allies. Britain on the other hand always seemed to be 'trying to hold them back or give them advice which seems to end in them not being able to do what they want to do'. There was a suspicion in the Pentagon and State Department about 'the possibility of us doing another Munich'. Lloyd now suggested a change of direction to Macmillan. 'Should we not now try to make the same sort of effort with France as we did in 1957 with United States?' he asked. 'Our assets are your personal relationship with General de Gaulle, the underlying French fear of Germany, and the fact that we do not really object to tripartite consultation which they want.'[9]

Macmillan's private secretary, Philip de Zulueta, noted for him that the question 'bristles with difficulties but the central one seems to be how to persuade the French to WANT us to take part in Europe. At the moment I do not think they want us at all.'[10] To Macmillan the answer had been clear for months: the forthcoming summits would offer a wonderful opportunity to 'use my old friendship with de Gaulle [...] to restore our old relations with France without disloyalty to the Americans'.[11]

*

Macmillan's first opportunity to use this friendship with de Gaulle came in March 1960 when he visited the French president at Rambouillet. Ambassador Jebb had advised against the trip and feared that Macmillan might 'be regarded as running after the General much too much'.[12] Macmillan, however, wanted to convince de Gaulle that 'Great Britain is a European power. [...] The Anglo-American association is not exclusive. [...] We would like to see a revived Europe, led by France with the UK at her side and with both countries contributing all their assets to what could become the central Western bastion.'[13]

Talks at Rambouillet were on a small scale and informal. Macmillan told de Gaulle that 'the United Kingdom would like to see a renascent Europe led by France'. Tripartite relations should be enhanced and frequent meetings held between the US, UK and French heads of government. The General concurred, but remained sceptical about relations with 'Les Anglaises'. 'The United Kingdom was always unwilling to choose between being part of Europe and having a special connection with the United States,' he noted.[14]

On the forthcoming summit, de Gaulle was uncharacteristically optimistic about reaching a *modus vivendi* on Berlin. 'Khrushchev has presented himself so much as the man of Peace that he will not want an absolutely barren summit,' de Gaulle predicted.[15] The West should be firm during the initial stages of the summit in order to win a final compromise at the end of the meeting to exploit Khrushchev's need for some kind of agreement. The General also suggested that the West should offer Khrushchev economic aid, which might 'help to civilise the Russians and encourage their development into a more bourgeois frame of mind'. This would also 'encourage them to accept the idea of a Concert of Great Powers to run the world'.[16]

De Gaulle's comment about a concert of powers to run the world complimented Macmillan's own hope for 'quiet meetings of four statesmen held in regular sequence in one or other of their capitals'.[17] Moreover, de Gaulle's suggestion that a com-promise should come at the end of a summit accorded with his own conclusion, drawn from the Jebb memorandum in February 1959, that they would find agreement only in a crisis.[18] When Macmillan returned to England, weary but optimistic, he believed he had succeeded in 'revitalising [an] old friendship'.[19] He told the Queen that 'I succeeded in convincing him that we wished to play our full part in Europe and to base our foreign policy on close and intimate co-operation with the French.'[20]

Macmillan hoped to consolidate the revitalisation of his relationship with de Gaulle during the general's state visit to England the following month. This was de Gaulle's first state visit to any country as president of the Fifth Republic. Appearances suggested that Anglo-French relations had indeed entered a new period of 'intimate co-operation'. De Gaulle paid lavish and genuine tributes to Britain and its people, most notably in his address to the Lords and MPs at Westminster. 'Heroic and alone, [Britain] took upon herself the liberty of the world,' he declared.[21]

The trip had a tremendous impact on de Gaulle. His memoirs recall the 'great splendour', with everything 'prepared in such a way as to ensure that the visit of General de Gaulle was some-thing out of the ordinary'. The visit might have been more appropriate for Louis XIV than for the president of a republic. Spectacular crosses of Lorraine lit with fireworks adorned the front of Buckingham palace. Trumpet fanfares sounded as de Gaulle arrived to address parliament. Crowds lined the streets as the General and the Queen rode together in an open carriage.[22] When the president arrived back at Orly airport after the trip, he drew aside Michael Hadow, the British embassy representative. 'I should like you to know how grateful I am for the magnificent arrangements in England by your government and the wonder-ful reception I was given', he said intensely. 'Everyone from the Queen ... to the people in the streets, showed marvellous friendship. It was, in truth, a very emotional experience.'[23] De Gaulle had come a long way since his first difficult days in London in 1940.

Despite de Gaulle's appreciation of British hospitality, Macmillan had been unable to use the visit to continue improving relations between the two governments. The president had turned down an invitation to visit Macmillan at Chequers, haughtily commenting that 'it would not be altogether appropriate in the course of a state visit'.[24] Brief conversations at Buckingham Palace were not encouraging. When de Gaulle asked outright if Britain would consider joining the Common Market, Macmillan simply replied that this was 'unfortunately impossible', but did not explain why.[25]

De Gaulle gave Macmillan an optimistic report on his talks the previous month with Khrushchev. The Soviet leader was 'a cunning, intelligent, self-made man' who 'knew the fundamentals of the matters under discussion very well'. Macmillan had concluded after his Moscow visit that 'Mr Khrushchev is *absolute* ruler of Russia and completely controls the situation'.[26] A year later, de Gaulle 'had been struck by the fact that Khrushchev was not by any means in the same position as Stalin'. He judged, perceptively, that 'Khrushchev's personal prestige was involved in getting some satisfaction for the Soviet Union out of détente'. He observed that:

> Mr Khrushchev talked a little differently when his advisers were present; no doubt this was because he knew that his conversation would be reported and he had certain rivals; Mr Khrushchev had to hold the Party; to some extent he was the prisoner of his own [...] propaganda.[27]

Macmillan confined himself to general expressions of hope that the summit would run smoothly and conviction that 'the West must be sincere'. They did not discuss substantive matters of principle and policy.[28] 'De G is certainly an extraordinary character,' Macmillan noted in his diary. 'Now that he is old (69) and mellowed, his charm is great. He speaks beautiful, rather old-fashioned French. He seemed quite impersonal and dis-interested.'[29]

If Macmillan's spirits remained buoyant after de Gaulle's visit to London, it was thanks to a breakthrough in an area of inter-national affairs that increasingly interested him. At the nuclear test ban talks in Geneva, the Soviets unexpectedly made concessions on meeting Western demands about inspection and, according to Lloyd, 'the possibility of a satisfactory agreement was in sight'.[30] Macmillan believed this was 'an opportunity to conclude an agree-ment which might be a turning point in the history of international negotiations on disarmament'. They had to make the US govern-ment 'appreciate the significance of this opportunity'. He urged that 'it must be made plain to them that we should find it very difficult to refrain from indicating publicly our readiness to accept an agreement on the lines now envisaged by the Russians'.[31]

When Macmillan wanted to make something 'plain' to the Americans, he invariably did it in the same way: by inviting himself to Washington. Speaking by telephone to Eisenhower on 21 March 1960, Macmillan asked if he might come over for the weekend to talk. They needed to discuss the test ban proposals, he told Eisenhower, adding that 'you would be the man in history to put an end to all this'.[32] Eisenhower was dubious as to whether his 'lame duck' period made agreement possible. He was clearly was unenthusiastic about the prospect of Macmillan paying a visit, but he could hardly refuse his old friend a few days at Camp David when de Gaulle would have a full state visit the following month. Eisenhower inquired if Macmillan would be bringing Selwyn Lloyd. Macmillan answered 'no', adding that he (the prime minister) 'would like to keep it quiet'.[33]

Lloyd had always been loyal to the prime minister, but was increasingly displaying his own policy ideas, particularly about relations with Europe and America. Days before Macmillan's trip to Washington, he wrote to the prime minister and suggested that a visit might be 'premature'. He feared the move would provide ammunition to those in Washington who believed US policy was 'being dictated to or fooled by the British'. By visiting the president now, he warned, Macmillan would be 'playing our ace too soon'.[34] In Washington, Herter predicted to the president that 'some friction [was] building up between Macmillan and Lloyd'.[35]

The prime minister left for Washington without his foreign secretary on 27 March to spend four days in the US. 'Ike received me with his usual charming grace,' Macmillan noted in his diary. 'He seemed really pleased to see me.'[36] Despite the summit being less than two months away, the subject was hardly raised during talks.[37] Macmillan's pre-visit brief had noted that 'the less detailed preparation that is done the better'.[38] In his diary, Macmillan wrote that 'the Summit must not be over-prepared but played by ear'.[39] Eisenhower, who seemed to agree, restricted himself to an expression of hope that 'we *should* be able to get some settlement on *Berlin*, if only we would guarantee to accept for ever the present frontiers of Germany (Oder-Neisse)'.[40]

A possible test ban treaty dominated official talks. 'The American plan is unexpectedly good', Macmillan recorded in his diary, and 'obviously represents a triumph for the State Department over the Pentagon and the Atomic Energy Committee'.[41] The president had 'had a very hard time about it and even had to threaten to resign'.[42] Although 'a lot of difficult points' remained to be worked out, Macmillan believed that 'if the Russians are sincere themselves and are convinced of our sincerity, a Treaty should be negotiable'.[43]

The official record reports the test ban treaty as the 'first object' of talks with Eisenhower. In reality, decisions of more immediate British national interest took place with the president agreeing to help Britain's nuclear weapons programme. As the prime minister informed the ministry of defence: 'In a desire to be of assistance in improving and extending the effective life of the V-Bomber force, the US ... is prepared to provide Skybolt missiles – minus warheads – to the UK on a rcimbursable basis in 1965 or thereafter.' As a trade-off for this favour, Macmillan agreed that 'in the same spirit of co-operation, the United Kingdom would be agreeable in principle to making the necessary arrangements for the United States Polaris tenders in Scottish ports'.[44] This decision to purchase nuclear weapons from the US brought with it significant financial savings consistent with the recommendations of 'Future Policy, 1960–1970.' The cost of buying from America was considerably less than any independently produced weapon; the US would bear the huge cost of research and development. Inevitably, the UK paid a different price: the move increased Britain's dependence on the United States and undermined the 'independent' aspirations of the 1957 Defence White Paper.[45]

Macmillan returned from Washington confident that he had put in place one of the first principles of 'Future Policy.' He wrote to the President that 'I believe that this last meeting had been one of the most fruitful which we have had together and I am so much comforted to feel that our thoughts are in line on so many subjects.'[46] By April 1960, Macmillan had good reason to feel optimistic about Britain's place on the world stage and his role as international statesman. The long-awaited summit was just a month away. Negotiations at Geneva looked set to produce agreement on a nuclear test ban. The Soviets were showing a genuine inclination towards easing cold war tensions. Most considered it unlikely that Khrushchev would sign a separate peace treaty with East Germany even if the summit failed to reach a settlement on Berlin.[47] Moscow was enjoying an 'American spring' with the Soviet leader even rumoured to be planning his own version of Disneyland depicting the great events of Soviet history.[48] Everything looked set for an important break-through at the Paris summit.

*

Detailed discussion about the Allied position for May had been taking place since the Western summit. Nicholas Henderson, the foreign office representative on the East-West working group in Paris, had complained about the 'slow and frustrating machinery of tripartite negotiations', but in despite of the difficulties, each working party produced a report for consideration by the foreign ministers in April.[49] With a month to go before the four heads of government would meet in Paris, high-level discussions finally began on how to concert an Allied position.

At meetings of the Western foreign ministers in Washington on 12–14 April, discussion on the mechanics of the summit took up considerable time. Macmillan, remembering his own time as foreign secretary, had made clear to Lloyd his view that 'the most important thing is to avoid a repetition of the last Geneva meeting when there were a great number of people present throughout and the four heads of government spent their time making propaganda speeches'. Whilst detailed negotiation would be co-ordinated by the foreign ministers, 'in the last resort agreements will probably only be brought to finality by the heads of government themselves'. Consequently, 'the Heads cannot confine their meetings only to discussion; they will have to negotiate as well'. Thus whilst 'the normal pattern should be meetings of perhaps three or four a side (heads of government, foreign ministers and one or two note takers each) … the final decisions might be made at meetings of the Heads only if this seems appropriate'.[50]

Selwyn Lloyd agreed that 'the paramount consideration should be to avoid a repetition of the last Geneva summit', but was anxious to preserve his own position. Writing to ambassador Caccia, who was to meet Herter and Couvé de Murville in Washington, Lloyd instructed:

> You should say that I feel strongly that the foreign ministers should be present at the substantial business meetings each day. The uncertainty as to what happened at Rambouillet

between the three heads of government should be an object lesson to us. It would be much more dangerous if that sort of thing happened after a meeting with Khrushchev. It would also be a frightful waste of time and effort if we have to spend the whole day trying to find out what actually happened between the heads of government, arguing over whose record was right etc.[51]

Not surprisingly, Couvé and Herter welcomed Lloyd's desire to keep the foreign ministers seriously involved. It also found favour with Eisenhower.

The president had written to Macmillan in March that 'I never lose my conviction that sooner or later in some fashion or other, we shall bring about some rift in the clouds.'[52] In mid-April, when General de Gaulle completed his round of discussions with all the participants of the summit by paying a visit to Washington, Eisenhower told him it would be 'a splendid exit for me to end up, without any sacrifice of principle, with an agreement between East and West!'[53] Eisenhower's biographer, Stephen Ambrose, suggests the president's 'own desire to make a breakthrough in the arms race, as his final act as a world leader, was greater than ever. [...] Eisenhower was ready to take some risks and make some concessions.'[54] Yet for all his supposed zeal about ending his presidency with a breakthrough at the summit, Eisenhower proved to be more than a little diffident about getting involved.

During discussions between the foreign ministers in Washington, Herter revealed that if the summit went beyond 23 May, Vice-President Nixon would replace Eisenhower, who had to leave for an official visit to Lisbon. Herter's colleagues were astonished. It was common knowledge that Khrushchev and Nixon held a personal dislike for each other. During their meetings in the Soviet Union and USA, serious antipathy had developed, not helped by Nixon's wish to portray himself as 'tough' on communism.[55] If the summit had been progressing well, the arrival of Nixon might break the atmosphere. If things were going badly, no-one seemed more likely to heighten tension. When Khrushchev heard of the idea, he angrily noted that sending Nixon to a peace conference was 'like putting a goat in charge of a cabbage patch'. Was this, he inquired, the action of a president who wanted genuine accord at Paris?[56]

Eisenhower showed similar insensitivity when it came to the question of negotiation. Macmillan had told Lloyd that 'the Heads […] will have to negotiate as well', but Eisenhower was not convinced. He agreed that the heads of government should meet for a restricted session at Paris but maintained that this should be for discussion and not negotiation. This would allow the leaders to talk more freely, leaving to the foreign ministers the task of using the talks as a basis for the detailed negotiations.[57] Even on the social side of the summit, Eisenhower seemed unwilling to play. Harold Caccia reported impatiently on a rambling tripartite meeting at which the only topic of discussion was the president's refusal to attend cocktail parties.

Macmillan was concerned about Eisenhower's reluctance to take a pro-active role at the summit, but his alarm was greater about the West's incoherent negotiating position. The foreign ministers at their meetings on 12–14 April approved the lacklustre working party reports.[58] After four months of intensive negotiation, the foreign office reluctantly conceded that 'there has been virtually no change since the Western heads of government discussed Berlin and Germany in Paris in December'.[59] Macmillan wrote to Freddie Bishop, his former private secretary, the summit briefing book 'makes pretty depressing reading since it is clear that very little advance is contemplated by most of my colleagues'.[60] The foreign office had been bogged 'down in all this paper and NATO has got mixed up too'. He predicted that 'if there is to be some break-through we shall have to do something dramatic ourselves'.[61]

In fact, the drama would come from elsewhere.

*

On 1 May 1960, Eisenhower's friend and closest adviser, Andrew Goodpaster, telephoned the president. 'One of our reconnaissance planes on a scheduled flight from its base in Turkey, is overdue and possibly lost', he reported. Early the following morning, Goodpaster, his face 'an etching of bad news', informed the president that 'I have received word from the CIA that the U–2 reconnaissance plane I mentioned yesterday is still missing. The pilot reported an engine flameout at a position about thirteen hundred miles inside Russia and has not been heard from since. With the amount of fuel he had on board, there is not a chance of his still being aloft'. Eisenhower recalled that 'I knew instantly that this was one of our U–2 planes, probably over Russia'. This was the beginning of a sorry tale of bad luck, miscalculation and sheer incompetence at the highest level.[62]

Since the beginning of the cold war, the USA had made continual attempts to conduct aerial espionage over the territory of the Soviet Union. By February 1955, the Lockheed Skunkworks had built a plane that would fly at more than 70,000 feet for 4000 miles. Built of titanium, the Utility–2 (U–2) was so light that test pilots later dubbed it the world's first disposable aeroplane.[63] The following year Eisenhower gave his approval for the first violation of Soviet air space by the new spy plane. The CIA would control individual missions, but each series of flights had to win the president's permission.[64]

The CIA had recognised the danger of a spy plane being shot down over Russia and had taken precautions to ensure that in the event there would be no proof of espionage. The plane was so light and fragile, thought the CIA's Richard Bissell, that there was only 'one chance in a million' that it would survive a hit. Moreover, for that 'one chance', an explosive device had been implanted that would fire automatically should the pilot use his ejector seat. The pilot himself had a hollow silver dollar, which contained a poison pin – the flyers were advised but not ordered to use it should they come down in the Soviet Union. Everyone assumed that if a U–2 were lost, the pilot would not survive.[65]

Eisenhower had always been sensitive to the political implications of the U–2 missions. He stopped them before Khrushchev's visit to America and, according to the CIA's Richard Bissell, no flights were authorised in 1959 after the Camp David talks.[66] There is some confusion as to whether Khrushchev raised the question of U–2 flights with Eisenhower during their private talks. The CIA's Raymond Garthoff later confirmed that the agency had expected Khrushchev to introduce the matter. He 'did not know for certain' whether the issue was discussed, but 'it is possible that the conversation on this point was especially private and the president did not allow Goodpaster to speak of it'. Whether or not the matter was raised, 'after Camp David, the president was especially cautious'.[67]

Early in 1960, CIA chief Allen Dulles had asked Eisenhower for permission to resume U–2 flights into Soviet territory. It was vital, he claimed, that the CIA look at the Inter-Continental Ballistic Missile launch sites in the Northern Urals and near the White Sea.[68] Eisenhower knew that renewing U–2 flights might be 'prejudicial to the kind of improvement we were working toward with the Soviets', but considered this a risk worth taking if it resulted in more information about ICBMs. On 9 April, for the first time since Camp David and just a month before the summit, a U–2 spy plane flew into Soviet airspace.[69]

When the military informed Khrushchev that the Americans had sent a spy plane over Soviet territory, he was horrified. Charles Bohlen acutely observed that the flight was 'almost [a] personal insult' to Khrushchev:

> I think it made him out as a fool. He'd been telling obviously all the other leaders that Eisenhower was a good, solid guy and you could trust him, and then – whambo – this plane comes over, and this shook a lot of Khrushchev's authority in the Soviet Union.[70]

Yet, in spite of all the difficulties the flight caused him, Khrushchev remained silent. There was no diplomatic protest – formal or informal. Thus, when Dulles came to Eisenhower to ask for another flight, the president expected that Khrushchev would turn another blind eye.

Eisenhower's risk proved to be a fatal miscalculation. At 06:26 on 1 May, Francis Gary Powers took off from the Peshawar airfield in Turkey. An hour later, his U–2 plane entered Soviet airspace. Georgi Aleksandrovitch Mikhailov, a colonel on duty at the central Headquarters of the Air Defence Department (ADD) later recalled the dramatic moment of impact:

> The target approached the zone of anti-aircraft rockets in the area of Sverdlovsk. There followed the command to destroy the target. The first rocket brought down Powers. The rocket was armed with a detonator that exploded some 10 metres from the plane. The plane was damaged by the explosion, the engine jammed, the pilot's seat moved. Powers could not eject. When he finally got out he had lost height from 22,000m to 6,000m. He jumped with a parachute and a few seconds later a second rocket hit the plane.[71]

Khrushchev waited until 5 May to make his first public comment about the U–2. 'I must report to you on aggressive action against the Soviet Union in the past few weeks by the United States of America', he told more than 1,300 Deputies crowded into the White Hall of the Kremlin Palace. 'What was this?' enquired the Chairman to cheering, 'a Mayday greeting?'[72] Nevertheless, having delivered his account of the U–2 mission in bellicose terms, Khrushchev changed tone to give Eisenhower an exit. 'Who sent this aircraft across the Soviet frontier?' he asked. 'Was it the American Commander-in-Chief who, as everyone knows, is the President? Or was this aggressive act performed by Pentagon militarists without the President's knowledge?' It was these latter American 'hawks' not Eisenhower, he suggested, who were trying to 'torpedo the Paris summit'.[73]

The State Department responded blithely to questions by reporters on Khrushchev's speech by saying that a weather plane had gone missing over Turkey. 'It may be that this was the missing plane [... and] that having a failure in the oxygen equipment, this could result in the pilot losing consciousness, the plane continuing on automatic pilot for a considerable distance and accidentally violated Soviet airspace.'[74] NASA issued a comprehensive statement offering a full, detailed, but dishonest account of the U–2 mission. It gave false details of route, flight time, altitude and mission purpose. Douglas Dillon at the State Department later recalled 'this statement was absolutely crazy because we *knew* the Russians would jump us on it'.[75]

By the evening of 5 May, the full extent of the debacle was slowly unravelling. At a Moscow drinks party, US Ambassador Thompson overheard Soviet deputy foreign minister, Jacob Malik, comment that his government was 'still questioning the pilot'. On his return to the embassy, Thompson fired off an emergency telegram warning the State Department not to issue a press release that Powers could contradict. The telegram arrived in Washington at 1:34pm, two minutes into the detailed briefing given by NASA.[76] Two days later, Khrushchev announced that 'we have the pilot, who is quite alive and kicking!'[77] He went on to outline the whole story – Power's name and unit, his mission, the poison pin – and produced photographs taken from the U–2. Yet still Eisenhower had an escape route. 'I am quite willing', Khrushchev declared, 'to grant that the president knew nothing about the fact that such a plane was sent into the Soviet Union'.[78]

The Soviets had caught the United States red-handed. The Eisenhower administration looked extremely foolish. Not only had it behaved stupidly in sending a spy plane into Soviet airspace immediately before a summit, it had bungled that operation and created a ridiculous lie to cover the failure. Now according to the Soviet leader, it seemed that the president did not even run his own government. Nevertheless, the situation was not yet beyond redemption. Ambassador Thompson had noted his belief that Khrushchev's behaviour still suggested he did not want to 'slam any doors'.[79] In private, the Soviet leader continued to look for a way out. At a party in the Czech embassy, he identified the CIA as a suitable scapegoat for the U–2 mission. Pulling the US ambassador to one side, Khrushchev implored him: 'This U–2 thing has put me in a terrible spot. You have to get me off it.'[80]

Eisenhower's personal secretary, Ann Whitman, recorded on 9 May that the president was 'very depressed' about 'the matter of the spy in sky'. He even confided to her that 'I would like to resign'.[81] The humiliation was almost too much to bear. The *New York Times* reported national anger and dismay sweeping across the nation. Western European capitals were 'stunned'.[82] By the afternoon, Whitman noted, the president had 'bounced back with his characteristic ability to accept the bad news, not dwell on it, and so go ahead'.[83] He told members of the National Security Council:

> Well, we're just going to have to take a lot of beating on this – and I'm the one, rightly, who's going to have to take it. [...] Of course, one had to expect that the thing would fail at one time or another. But that it had to be such a boo-boo and that we would be caught with our pants down was rather painful.[84]

Admonishing all officials to remain silent about the subject, he concluded 'we will now just have to endure the storm'.[85] Vice-President Nixon urged Herter to 'get away from this "little boy in the cookie jar" posture'. It was embarrassing 'to leave the president in the posture where he says he doesn't know anything about this; to give that impression would be to imply that war could start without the president's knowledge'.[86]

Finally, on 11 May, Eisenhower went on the record. 'No-one wants another Pearl Harbor,' the president began, which meant that 'we must have knowledge of military forces and preparations around the world, especially those capable of massive surprise attack'. The Soviet 'fetish of secrecy and concealment' demanded that information had to be gathered 'in every feasible way' to protect against surprise attack. These activities 'have their own rules and methods of concealment which seek to mislead and obscure'. Such measures were 'a distasteful but vital necessity'. Nevertheless, Eisenhower concluded:

> We must not be distracted from the real issues of the day by what is an incident or symptom of the world situation today. The real issues are the ones we will be working on at the summit – disarmament, the search for solutions affecting Germany and Berlin, and the whole range of East-West relations, including the reduction of secrecy and suspicion. Frankly, I am hopeful that we may make progress on these great issues.[87]

After such a bullish and unrepentant statement, the president's appeal for 'progress' at the summit was little more than wishful thinking. The CIA's Allen Dulles, a man with his own fetish for secrecy, wearily reflected on the whole mess: 'We should have kept quiet'.[88]

Chapter Six

A great and tragic event

MAY 1960

'QUITE A PLEASANT Saturday', Macmillan recorded in his diary on 8 May. 'The Commonwealth in pieces and the summit doomed!'[1] He had managed to postpone the inevitable expulsion of apartheid-ridden South Africa from the Commonwealth that spring, but attempts to diffuse the U–2 crisis were more problematic. The Powers flight, he later recorded, provided the 'opening stages of a drama which, in spite of periods of comedy and even farce, ended tragically'. Within ten days, 'the grand edifice which I had worked so long and so painfully to build seemed totally and finally destroyed'.[2]

Eisenhower had decided not to tell Macmillan about the downing of the spy plane. The prime minister only found out by reading Khrushchev's speech. 'The Americans have created a great folly', he recorded in his diary:

> The Russians have got the machine; the cameras; a lot of the photographs – and the pilot. God knows what he will say when tortured! […] The President, State Dept, and Pentagon have all told separate and conflicting stories, and are clearly in a state of panic. Khrushchev has made two very amusing and effective speeches, attacking the Americans for spying incompetently and lying incompetently too. He

may declare the Summit off. Or the Americans may be stung into doing so.[3]

Macmillan suggested to the American State Department that the US follow British procedures by simply refusing to discuss intelligence matters in public. When the US finally admitted to espionage activities, Macmillan found it all to be 'a very odd story'. Eisenhower seemed to be 'quite distracted and without any clear plan'. Eisenhower's mishandling of events shocked Macmillan:

> Khrushchev might well have accepted either silence or some formal disclaimer. Unhappily, with characteristic honesty, Eisenhower stated, at a press conference, that the U–2 flights had been made with his knowledge and approval. Although on the same day, 11 May, Khrushchev had stated publicly that he expected the summit to take place and even on his arrival in Paris issued a moderate statement, yet it was clear that the hardening of the Soviet line was largely due to Eisenhower's unlucky admission.[4]

Omitted from Macmillan's memoirs are sensitive diary references to British U–2 espionage flights. 'We actually have done some very successful ones (with airplanes which the Americans gave us)', he noted. 'We call the exercise "Oldster". But, with the Summit negotiations coming on, all ours have been cancelled by my orders.'[5] Doubtless Macmillan would have agreed with de Gaulle that sending in a spy plane so close to the summit would be 'an absurdly ill-timed violation of Soviet air space'.[6] Nevertheless, Macmillan felt considerable relief that 'nothing has yet come out about the British flights into Russia'.[7]

Philip de Zulueta believed that the U–2 incident might work in favour of the West: with Khrushchev's present need to pacify 'hard-liners' in the Soviet Union, the capture of Powers allowed the Russian leader to be tough before rather than at the summit.[8] Ambassador Patrick Reilly was less optimistic. The U–2 affair, he reported, had afforded Khrushchev a 'wonderful propaganda windfall. [...] It had swung public opinion behind him, so that the West could possibly be blamed for failure at the summit'.[9] Macmillan had written to Khrushchev on 10 May that 'in spite of the difficulties, I am hopeful that we shall make progress', but when he left for Paris on 15 May, he did so 'full of apprehension'.[10] The summit might still take place, but no one had the slightest idea what would happen there. 'The summit would not be a Sunday school picnic,' Eisenhower coolly told the National Security Council.[11]

To British journalists, however, the U–2 incident confirmed suspicions that Eisenhower lacked the intellectual qualities to be president. 'Such alarms are part of the game of bluff and double bluff sometimes considered a proper introduction to peace talks,' intoned the *Daily Mail*. 'Both America and Russia have been playing this game. Khrushchev is better at it. He can run rings round the honest, likeable but slower witted soldier in the White House, as the last few days have shown.[12] *The Times* endorsed this view. Eisenhower had been 'foolish in the extreme' and had 'handed Mr Khrushchev a propaganda triumph on a plate'.[13]

Yet in reality, the U–2 incident had been a disaster too for Khrushchev. Khrushchev had staked a considerable amount of his own prestige on a successful summit. After the Camp David meetings with Eisenhower, the Soviet Premier had emphasised his personal relationship with the president. Eisenhower, he insisted, was a man to be trusted. Ambassador Thompson later concluded that 'Khrushchev's own deepest desire [was] to gain time for the forthcoming triumphs of Soviet economic progress. For this he really wants a generally unexplosive period in foreign affairs.'[14] The military, backed by Kremlin hardliners and Peking, was pushing for increased armaments build-up and bitterly resented Khrushchev's plans for rationalisation. His policy of co-existence had secured very little in the way of real accord. Fighting a rear-guard action against those demanding an aggressive encouragement of world revolution, Khrushchev needed results. The U–2 incident, however, insured the reversal of this policy. 'From the time Gary Powers was shot down in a U–2 over the Soviet Union, I was no longer in full control,' Khrushchev would later say. 'Those who felt that America had imperialist intentions and that military strength was the most important thing had the evidence they needed, and when the U–2 incident occurred, I no longer had the ability to overcome that feeling.'[15]

The British came closest to recognizing this at the time. At a meeting the day before the summit, Selwyn Lloyd finally asked Herter outright what had gone wrong during the U–2 incident. The secretary of state conceded that 'a lot of silly things' had been said and, in retrospect, wished that a traditional British 'silence' on these matters had been adopted. However, following the initial 'stupid story', which he casually blamed on press secretary James Hagerty, the administration 'had felt they had to tell the truth'.[16] Lloyd was not a great policy innovator, but he was extremely perspicacious when judging moods. 'Mr Khrushchev would feel that he had been let down in the eyes of his own people as he had told them that President Eisenhower was a man of peace,' he told the complacent secretary of state. The president and Mr Khrushchev, he warned, 'must have this out by themselves, otherwise the incident would hang over the conference'. Herter was unmoved. Eisenhower had considered raising the matter with Khrushchev, but the final US position was that it was best to 'wait for Mr Khrushchev to raise it; the president would then suggest a talk between the two of them'. Given Khrushchev's sensitivity to traditional courtesies, this decision not to take the initiative on the subject was a serious misjudgement.[17]

Despite Selwyn Lloyd's sense of foreboding about the forthcoming summit, a general atmosphere of excitement and expectation had emerged. It was springtime in Paris. Everyone in the French capital was in party mood. With politics in vogue, the British embassy became *the* fashionable place to be and to be seen. Under the direction of raffish Sir Gladwyn Jebb, hospitality was sophisticated and generous. In particular, much was made of the cases of vintage claret that Jebb was rumoured to have bought for consumption during the summit. To everyone's disappointment, the ambassador's claret would remain unopened.

*

President Eisenhower arrived at Orly Airport, Paris, on 15 May to declare that 'the hopes of humanity call on the four of us to purge our minds of prejudice and our hearts of rancour.' Then with a conspicuous lack of goodwill, he concluded that it would be 'a pleasure to meet again with my old friends President de Gaulle and prime minister Macmillan'.[18] Khrushchev later complained to Macmillan that 'Mr Eisenhower seemed to have forgotten that at Camp David he had addressed him as his friend.'[19]

Khrushchev had arrived at Orly the previous day promising to 'exert all efforts to make the conference a success'.[20] In reality, he recorded later, 'my anger was building up inside me like an electric force which could be discharged in a great flash at any moment'.[21] He had won approval from Kremlin colleagues to fly early to Paris in order to sort out the U–2 debacle with Eisenhower before the summit began. It seems likely that Khrushchev attended the Paris meeting only on the condition that the United States apologised publicly for its violation of Soviet airspace. To ensure that Khrushchev maintained this position, a 'minder' kept him company. Marshal Malinovsky was unenthusiastic about detente, deeply resentful of Khrushchev's proposed rationalisation of the military, and furious at the humiliation inflicted by four years of U–2 intrusions. His limpet-like presence to Khrushchev would ensure that the Soviet premier had little or no chance for an informal quiet word with Eisenhower.

Yet not all was lost. Khrushchev had to win his apology from Eisenhower, but he was determined do so without humiliating him. On the morning of 15 May, Khrushchev called on President de Gaulle, accompanied by Gromyko and Malinovsky (whom de Gaulle amusingly called the 'rocket marshal'). He was in a belligerent mood. He warned that he would not attend the conference unless Eisenhower made a public apology condemning the aggression, announcing measures to punish its instigators, and giving his word not to repeat such actions. 'It was clear that the Soviets wanted either to inflict a spectacular humiliation on the United States or to extricate themselves from a conference which they now no longer desired after having clamoured so loudly for it,' de Gaulle later recalled.[22] Surely Khrushchev 'could not seriously expect' Eisenhower to apologise in this way, de Gaulle asked.[23] 'Espionage is undoubtedly a deplorable practice', he suggested, 'but how can it be avoided when two rival powers, heavily over-armed, give each other the impression that they may reach for their guns at any moment?'[24]

Khrushchev's attitude that morning led de Gaulle to conclude that the summit was as good as over. Macmillan's own talks with the Soviet leader in the evening offered a glimmer of hope. He asked Khrushchev if he would agree to meet the president. 'If Mr Eisenhower showed an interest in such an interview, he was ready to meet him,' the Soviet premier responded. However, he continued, if American policy continued to rest on a 'bandit's philosophy', the Soviet Union 'could not accept this'. Throughout their talk, Macmillan thought Khrushchev 'personally quite agreeable', but he 'did not succeed in appeasing him'. Macmillan's gloomy conclusion was that 'we're in for trouble' [25]

During the early evening of 15 May, Macmillan met Eisenhower and de Gaulle, to impress upon them that 'we must work to prevent the conference from breaking down before it has even started'. At his meeting with Khrushchev, he had been surprised to notice that the Soviet leader had 'looked towards Marshal Malinovsky and Mr Gromyko in a way unusual for him'. He continued:

> Perhaps the truth of the matter was that Mr Khrushchev had been in some difficulty in his own country in carrying on with the policy of a détente. He had referred very kindly to President Eisenhower. Mr Khrushchev had staked his reputation on his success in reducing tension and he might have been a good deal criticised. [...] Mr Khrushchev might try to see President Eisenhower and perhaps in view of Mr Khrushchev's remarks about US determination to continue the flights a face saving formula could be found.[26]

With Macmillan pushing Eisenhower to talk to the Soviet premier and General de Gaulle cautiously agreeing 'to President Eisenhower meeting Mr Khrushchev separately', the initiative passed to the American leader. Eisenhower faced two questions: first, would he meet Khrushchev bilaterally, and, second, could he find the sophistry to give both sides an honourable way out of the U–2 affair?

Eisenhower 'doubted whether it was now possible to meet Mr Khrushchev bilaterally' for the rather bizarre reason that 'then he and Mr Khrushchev might have different versions of what occurred to tell the other two'. On Khrushchev's demands for a promise that nothing like the U–2 would occur again, Eisenhower was implacable. He was only 'ready to say that he had not asserted that flights would continue'. Although he would admit that 'flights were illegal and wrong', he maintained that the United States had the right to 'protect themselves'.[27] Eisenhower later recalled he told them plainly that 'I would not permanently tie the hands of the United States government for the single purpose of saving a conference.[28]

The president disliked logic-chopping arguments and weasel words. This straightforwardness had impressed Khrushchev the previous summer. However, if Eisenhower was genuinely committed to keeping the summit alive, his diplomatic skills now failed him in Paris. First, he handed Khrushchev the initiative from the outset by rejecting the advice of Macmillan (strongly put) and de Gaulle (less so) to seek a bilateral meeting with the Soviet premier. Second, when finally he did meet Khrushchev face-to-face, he offered an apology that was so arrogant and petty that he must have known Khrushchev would be unable to accept it.

John Foster Dulles, the former secretary of state, always emphasised to Eisenhower the dangers of playing at summitry.[29] The president was not a professional diplomat, he had warned, adding that it would be difficult to concert and enforce a unified Western standpoint in the face of a monolithic Soviet negotiating team. The Soviets would exploit differences in the Western camp to utilise them for propaganda purposes. 'I didn't think any more of them [summits] than he did, except I thought once in a while they couldn't hurt, and they might do something useful – particularly as far as public opinion was concerned', Eisenhower had observed of this view.[30] Now as he sat down with Macmillan and de Gaulle in Paris, the president, not for the first time, must have reflected on how much he missed his skilled and protective lieutenant.[31]

At final discussions before meeting Khrushchev, the Western leaders could agree on almost nothing. The deliberations of working parties and foreign ministers had produced very little in the way of positive suggestions. After Eisenhower had pointed to 'certain differences' between the leaders on disarmament, Berlin and Germany, de Gaulle plaintively asked whether 'in that case, could the West propose nothing?' The best plan was to wait for Khrushchev to suggest something.

Whereas de Gaulle and Eisenhower were preaching resolute inactivity, Macmillan was already 'flying kites' about Berlin, giving de Gaulle and Eisenhower an early impression of British weakness. West Berlin as 'a free city under the United Nations', the prime minister casually noted, 'might not be such a terrible thing. It was not like agreeing to annihilate Berlin'. Obviously, a summit could not ratify a 'free city' idea, but it could be set as the final aim of two years' talking. De Gaulle retorted that this was tantamount to accepting the Soviet plan. Hastily back-tracking, Macmillan said that 'the most important thing was to secure a period of two years in which to talk about a solution'.[32]

When Macmillan retired that evening, he reflected in his diary that 'No-one quite knew what to do or how it would develop'. He noted that 'De Gaulle was pretty sure that Khrushchev would press it to the point of rupture'. On the other hand, 'Eisenhower was not convinced.' Thus Macmillan went to his bed that night with 'rather a heavy heart, but not without hope'.[33]

*

Macmillan woke at 7:15am on 16 May. He had slept badly. That day, he later recalled, would be 'one of the most agonising as well as exhausting which I have ever been through except perhaps in battle'. Within forty-five minutes, Macmillan was in the US embassy, sharing breakfast with Eisenhower. He found the president 'depressed and uncertain'. The conversation was 'rather strained'. Eisenhower 'still didn't know what to do'. As Macmillan fussed over his boiled egg, he tried to remain cheerful, con-cluding that 'the only thing was to make the best of things together'.[34] Within the hour, all hope of this had disappeared.

Around 9am, Eisenhower gave Macmillan sight of his opening statement to the conference. The PM was horrified. 'It was *not* very good and much too truculent,' he recorded in his diary. 'Nor did it make it at all clear whether the Americans still claimed the right to make these flights (contrary to international law) or whether they were going to stop them.'[35] Macmillan was unusually frank to the president about his reservations. An argument quickly flared up. As the row intensified, Eisenhower was joined by Herter and then by a growing number of officials including Merchant, Bohlen and Thompson. 'There was great confusion, and some bitterness,' Macmillan wrote. 'The Americans were in considerable disarray.' When he departed for the Elysée Palace to attend the first meeting of the four leaders, the prime minister knew in his heart that the summit was already over.[36]

At 11am, the heads of government took their places at the conference table. It would be the only time they sat down together in Paris. It was also the last time that Britain would participate in a full working summit meeting of the wartime Great Powers.[37] President de Gaulle, who as host was co-ordinating the meeting, began by referring to the document that Khrushchev had circulated. Knowing that Eisenhower had a prepared statement to make, de Gaulle then asked if anyone would like to comment on that text.

Events took a turn for the worse almost immediately. As Eisenhower opened his mouth to speak, Khrushchev leapt to his feet proclaiming: 'I would like the floor.' Eisenhower, startled, said that he too would like to make a statement. Would Mr Khrushchev mind, de Gaulle inquired, if Eisenhower spoke first? 'I was the first to ask for the floor and I would like my request to be granted,' Khrushchev replied. De Gaulle looked to Eisenhower, who gave weary consent.[38] 'With a gesture reminiscent of Mr Micawber,' Macmillan recorded in his diary, Khrushchev 'pulled a large wad of folio typewritten papers out of his pocket and began to speak.' The statement was violent, bitter and personal. He lost the thread of his speech and frequently repeated himself. With his indignation growing, Khrushchev's voice gradually crescendoed to a shout, drawing from de Gaulle the dry put-down: 'the acoustics in this room are excellent. We can all hear the Chairman.'[39]

Khrushchev's earlier statements had implied that if the Americans apologised, the summit might still proceed. He now made it clear that the summit was over. 'The Soviet Union is not renouncing efforts to achieve agreement', he told the meeting, 'and we are sure that reasonable agreements are possible, but, evidently, not at this but at another time':

> Therefore, we think that some time should be allowed to elapse so that the questions that have arisen should settle and so that those responsible for the determining of the policies of a country would analyse what kind of responsibility they placed upon themselves having declared an aggressive course in their relations with the Soviet Union and other Socialist countries. Therefore we would think that there is no better way out than to postpone the conference of the heads of government for approximately six to eight months.[40]

The suggestion was a blatant insult. Khrushchev was saying there would be no summit until America elected a new president. He was sorry 'this meeting has been torpedoed by the reactionary circles of the United States' but, he continued, 'let the disgrace and responsibility for this rest with those who have proclaimed a bandit policy towards the Soviet Union'.[41]

If it was not obvious already that Khrushchev was attacking Eisenhower personally, the Chairman went on to offer an even greater insult that would make it embarrassingly clear. Turning to Eisenhower's forthcoming visit to the USSR, Khrushchev noted that the 'provocative and aggressive actions' of the US had deprived the USSR 'of a possibility to receive the president with proper cordiality'. Conditions were 'clearly unfavourable for this visit'. He continued:

> That is why we believe that at present the visit of the president of the United States to the Soviet Union should be postponed and agreement should be reached as to the

time of the visit when the conditions for the visit would be mature.

He finished snidely that 'I believe that both President Eisenhower and the American people will understand me correctly'.[42]

Macmillan recorded in his diary that 'Khrushchev had tried to pulverise Ike (as Micawber did Heep) by a mixture of abuse, vitriolic and offensive, and legal argument. It must have lasted ... three quarters of an hour.' The whole routine was 'a most unpleasant performance' that was intended 'to be as offensive as possible to Eisenhower'.[43] As Khrushchev's speech progressed, Macmillan had observed that 'the president could scarcely contain himself'. 'We can't sit for this,' growled Bohlen to the president. 'I am going to take up smoking again' scribbled Eisenhower to Herter.[44]

Eisenhower's follow-up statement to the conference was short and unapologetic. Its peevishness had distressed Macmillan at breakfast that morning, but under the circumstances, it seemed to capture the mood. Terse and unrepentant, Eisenhower reiterated that 'the United States will not shirk its responsibility to safeguard against surprise attack'. Espionage remained a 'distasteful necessity ... in a world where nations distrust each other's intentions'. Khrushchev would do well to remember that 'not only the United States but most other countries are constantly the targets of elaborate and relentless espionage of the Soviet Union'. Eisenhower proposed that he and Khrushchev conduct bilateral discussions on the question of spying while the main conference proceeded. He had come to Paris 'to seek agreements with the Soviet Union which would eliminate the necessity for all forms of espionage, including overflights'. In the meantime the U–2 flights 'were suspended after the recent incident and are not to be resumed'.[45]

When Eisenhower sat down, it was Macmillan's turn to speak. He gave a jumpy performance that de Gaulle later recalled 'exuded anxiety and distress'.[46] Macmillan told the conference he 'deplored that after so long and painful ascent towards the summit it should be found to be so clouded'. Each side must now accept that 'what had happened had happened'. The Soviet leader had said he would not participate in a summit if over-flights continued. Surely he could see that 'the president had now made it absolutely clear that this was not American policy'. He was glad that Khrushchev only proposed to postpone the conference, but he might reflect on 'a French saying to the effect that what is postponed is lost'. Macmillan ended with a desperate plea for compromise. 'The eyes of the world were on the heads of government and hopes of the peoples of all countries rested on them,' he declared. It was his hope that after taking note of the declarations which had been made, they might proceed with their work.[47]

Macmillan had begged Khrushchev to reconsider; de Gaulle in contrast unleashed his disdainful temper. 'Before you left Moscow', he told him, 'I sent my ambassador to see you to ask whether this meeting should be held or should be postponed. You told my ambassador that this conference should be held and that it would be fruitful.' To call for a postponement now was the height of diplomatic discourtesy. 'You have brought Mr Macmillan here from London, General Eisenhower from the United States and have put me to serious inconvenience to organise and attend a meeting which your intransigence will make impossible.'[48] The summit meeting had been convened to alleviate tension that developed between East and West. Surely the U–2 incident 'made it all the more necessary that the talks should not be concluded without some steps being taken to bring about a détente'. The heads of government 'would not be living up to their responsibilities if they separated simply as a result of the incident. [...] The conference must go on.' To allow tempers to cool, he proposed a twenty-four hour recess, during which he would be willing to meet any of the other heads of government.[49]

De Gaulle had barely finished before Khrushchev again leapt to his feet. President Eisenhower's statement had contained 'no expression of regret'. Quite the contrary: it had implied that Eisenhower 'had approved what had happened and … sought to justify it'. 'This was unacceptable,' Khrushchev thundered. As to the president's 'Open Skies' proposals, until such time as disarmament could be made 'real and effective', then 'the Soviet sky would remain shut and they would shoot down anybody who ventured into it'.[50]

De Gaulle interjected. Why was Khrushchev making so much fuss about an unarmed espionage plane? 'Yesterday', he observed, 'a satellite you launched just before you left Moscow to impress us overflew the sky of France eighteen times without my permission. How do I know that you do not have cameras aboard which are taking pictures of my country.' Khrushchev protested that the Sputnik had no cameras. So how did Sputnik procure pictures of the far side of the moon, inquired de Gaulle? Because that one did have cameras, responded Khrushchev defensively. 'Ah,' said de Gaulle wryly, 'In *that* one you had cameras! Pray continue.'[51]

Wrong-footed, Khrushchev moved to reiterate his conditions for beginning the summit. He welcomed de Gaulle's proposal for a recess and was ready to begin talks as soon as 'the threat uttered against the Soviet Union [was] publicly repudiated'. In the meantime, he suggested, they might do well to take advantage of their surroundings: Paris was 'full of delightful chestnut groves which were particularly suitable for cool thinking'. Then, mixing genuine personal frustration with humbug, Khrushchev appealed to the other leaders:

> It was [his] earnest desire to put an end to the quarrel. If he might be permitted to use such language, he would like to ask what devil it was that had provoked the United States

government to such an act of provocation just before the summit. Had it not been for this act, the omens for the meeting would have been very favourable. When they had been together in United States, he and the president had called each other friends. But it was a poor sort of friendship which clashed in the sky. He raised his hands to the sky and God could see they were clean. His heart was also pure.[52]

Eisenhower later recalled that he almost choked on hearing Khrushchev's oath.[53]

Just after two o'clock, de Gaulle ended the meeting and suggested that 'there was nothing left to be done but for each one of those present to draw his own conclusions'.[54] The four leaders dispersed. They would never meet together again.

As Macmillan, Eisenhower and Khrushchev traipsed out, each disheartened and angry, de Gaulle caught the American president by the elbow: 'whatever happens', he told him, '*we are with you*'.[55] Later to aides, Eisenhower reflected that 'de Gaulle is quite a guy' and had 'really warmed his heart'.[56] After months of being a thorn in the president's flesh, de Gaulle had chosen this moment of crisis to offer unequivocal loyalty. When compared to this morale-boosting support, Macmillan's vacillation would look very bad to Eisenhower and his officials.

Storming into the American ambassador's residence, Eisenhower finally let his famous temper off its leash.[57] 'I'm just fed up! Fed up!' he shouted. That 'son-of-a-bitch' Khrushchev had been 'completely intransigent and insulting'. The Soviet premier had 'presented impossible demands' that were 'wholly unacceptable'. As to the withdrawn invitation to Moscow, that 'simply saved him the necessity of turning it down'.[58] 'We all felt the impact of the insults,' remembered Eisenhower's son, John: 'all harbouring strong resentment and bewilderment at Khrushchev's violent conduct'. Exhausted, the president retired to his bedroom to get some sleep.[59]

Just after 4pm, a statement was issued on Eisenhower's behalf which attacked the 'violence and inaccuracy' of Khrushchev's remarks at the opening conference session. American U–2 flights were not aggressive in nature, but protected the US against military threat. The use of such espionage activities was a 'distasteful necessity'. The US 'will not shirk its responsibility to safeguard against surprise attack'. Khrushchev had brushed aside reason that morning. By issuing a public ultimatum to the president, 'it was thus made apparent that he was determined to wreck the Paris conference'. That demand would 'never be acceptable' to the US. His conclusion on events so far was that Khrushchev had 'came all the way from Moscow to Paris with the sole intention of sabotaging this meeting on which so much of the hopes of the world have rested'.[60]

By the afternoon of 16 May, Macmillan, although gravely depressed, was preparing to make one last attempt to rescue the summit. 'There is no doubt it is a serious situation but I have not given up all hope' he wrote to Rab Butler in London. During the conference he had appealed to Khrushchev 'on the highest moral grounds', but the Soviet premier 'did not seem particularly impressed'. Although the leaders had failed to reach compromise at the conference table, Macmillan hoped to find it in the intimacy of private talks with Khrushchev, Eisenhower and de Gaulle.[61]

Macmillan's round of personal talks caused concern on several fronts. De Gaulle and Eisenhower were suspicious of Macmillan's intentions, believing that a summit opening with a Western capitulation would inevitably lead to a series of retreats. By searching for a compromise, Macmillan risked appearing vacillating and weak.[62] Even the foreign secretary and his foreign office aides mistrusted the prime minister's motives. They feared that, by going to see Khrushchev, allies would conclude that Macmillan was an appeaser. This fear was heightened by Macmillan's decision to take only de Zulueta, Freddie Bishop and Reilly to the meeting, leaving behind the beleaguered foreign secretary ('which annoyed me', complained Lloyd.) It had always been clear that the prime minister and his staff made foreign policy. Nevertheless, on no previous occasion had it been more apparent to Lloyd that his function was, in his own words, to follow the PM around 'making the occasional bleating noise'. Lloyd vented his frustration with the prime minister by attacking de Zulueta and Bishop. His anger provoked only contempt. Told that he would not be accompanying Macmillan to see Khrushchev, Lloyd protested in the strongest terms to de Zulueta and Bishop that this was 'government by private secretary'. The tart reply came back: 'Well, the only alternative is government by politician.'[63]

Before Macmillan went to visit Khrushchev, he called to see first de Gaulle and then Eisenhower. He found the French President in 'one of his cynical moods' and unwilling to entertain any hope of progress:

> De Gaulle said the whole thing was over and indeed that had been the opinion he had formed on the Sunday. [...] He felt convinced that Khrushchev had made up his mind by now on the line that he would take and had made this decision before coming to Paris.

De Gaulle cagily told Macmillan that some among his advisers, including the influential Debré, thought 'something might be done'. He bore Macmillan 'no ill-feeling' and was 'quite happy that I should make an effort with Mr Khrushchev'.[64]

If de Gaulle was obliging, Eisenhower was not. Loyal as ever to his old friend, Macmillan in his memoirs described Eisenhower as 'relaxed' at this meeting. At the time, however, he thought that the president was in fact 'very much shaken' by his experience with Khrushchev. Eisenhower told him that 'he had found it very difficult to keep his temper' that morning. With typical understatement, Macmillan recorded that Eisenhower had 'relieved the tension by expressing in quite idiomatic language what he had thought about Mr Khrushchev and the Russians'. Eisenhower was a blunt-speaking soldier. Whatever he said about Khrushchev, it was probably stronger than the 'he was a real S.O.B.' recorded by Macmillan in his memoirs.[65]

Behind Eisenhower's verbal attack on Khrushchev's character, Macmillan thought he detected 'a certain uneasiness'. He speculated about whether the collapse of the summit would affect the president's popularity. 'Although American opinion will rally to the president, there will have been and will be criticisms of the actual handling of the affair by the State Department and the president himself,' he reflected. 'Being a very sensitive man, he is conscious of this.'[66]

Given that Macmillan recognised Eisenhower's discomfort, he might have shown a little more sensitivity. For one who placed so much emphasis on the importance of personal relationships in diplomacy, Macmillan showed a considerable lack of judgement when speaking to the president on this occasion. Having denounced Khrushchev in the strongest possible terms, the president asked Macmillan what more he could do. He had 'gone a long way in his offer'. He could not 'condemn the action which he had authorised. [...] The demand for punishment was absurd.' Macmillan had a simple, if tactless, answer: 'I said I supposed he could "say he was sorry" – or, preferably [make] a formal diplomatic apology.' Always suspected by the Americans of weakness, Macmillan could not have said anything that was more likely to confirm that prejudice. Encouraged by his old friend to humiliate himself, the president could only reflect on de Gaulle's loyal promise that 'whatever happens, I want you to know that I am with you to the end'. De Gaulle was a difficult and irritating partner but in a real crisis, his support was unquestioned.[67] In comparison, Macmillan suddenly appeared a distinctly 'fair weather' friend.

By 9pm, Macmillan was exhausted. Aside from Lloyd's professional disapproval of Macmillan's round of visits that evening, he also thought the prime minister simply 'too tired' to see Khrushchev.[68] Nevertheless, Macmillan persevered, albeit without much success. Macmillan found Khrushchev 'polite, but quite unmovable'. Gromyko and the 'Rocket Marshal' sat-in on the meeting, stony-faced and silent.

Of course, Macmillan told the Soviet premier, he had 'quite understood what [he] had felt about the aircraft'. He recognised that 'it had been a great shock' and that Khrushchev had 'rightly and properly made his protest'. Now that Eisenhower had said the flights would not continue, 'might it be possible to sit down together and to go on with the business?' Obviously there would be a 'cloud over the meeting'. But if they were to go on for a few days then 'some foundations might have been laid' for a further discussions in six to eight months time. This would guarantee a 'sense of continuity'. If the conference broke up in acrimony, this continuity would be broken and public opinion alarmed. Surely Mr Khrushchev would agree that 'the great thing was to avoid a violent break?'[69]

After thanking Macmillan for his efforts and hinting that he knew the British too had sent planes into Soviet airspace, Khrushchev turned to the question of Eisenhower. Quite simply, he told Macmillan, 'he did not believe President Eisenhower and he did not think much of this American statement'. As to sending spy planes into Soviet territory, 'this was a perfidious policy which was coming to an end and which end would be hastened by the Soviet Union so that normal conditions could prevail in the world'. Surely Macmillan would admit that 'the United States had been caught red-handed'? Khrushchev was prepared to talk in Paris but only if Eisenhower apologised publicly and punished the 'guilty' men. If this did not happen, he would take no part in the conference.[70]

Khrushchev was brutal about Eisenhower. 'The difficulty was that President Eisenhower reigned but did not govern,' he suggested. Certainly 'he had some fine qualities, but political leaders must be judged by the acts which they did and the present situation was one in which the United States military gave President Eisenhower papers which he signed without reading them'. Khrushchev had little doubt that Allen Dulles conceived the plans for the U–2 flights.[71]

Undeterred by Khrushchev's contempt for Eisenhower, Macmillan continued to try to win round the Soviet premier. Mr Khrushchev, he believed, had made three demands: he wished the president to condemn the overflights, promise not to repeat them, and make that declaration publicly. Two of those three points were reasonable. But to ask a Head of State to 'condemn his own people' was asking too much:

> The president had gone further than the prime minister could remember any head of government having gone during his lifetime. Mr Khrushchev should take a broad view of this matter because the peace of the world was at stake. [...] All over the world small people were buoyed up with hope that the conference would succeed and he begged Mr Khrushchev to help find an honourable way to all to prevent disappointing these hopes.[72]

Leaving Khrushchev with this emotional appeal Macmillan left the Soviet embassy. Freed from the constraints of obsequious politeness, he dryly observed of the sartorially challenged Russians to de Zulueta: 'They might know how to make sputniks, but they certainly don't know how to make trousers.'[73] Joking apart, he hoped that Khrushchev 'would not act ... without seeing me again'.[74] As so often during those few days in Paris, Macmillan's hopes were quickly shattered.

*

At ten minutes past nine the following morning, a jovial Khrushchev gave an informal press conference whilst out walking the streets of Paris. In the Rue de Granule, he repeated his demand that America renounce its U–2 banditry, and confirmed that if this happened, the Soviets would participate in the summit. 'If not, we will leave for home,' he told reporters.[75] 'My hopes were rudely and rapidly dashed,' Macmillan noted despairingly. 'Mr K has given an informal press conference (at 9.25 am) in which he reiterated *all* his demands on the Americans.'[76]

Fifty minutes later, the three Western heads of government met at the Elysée Palace to discuss tactics. The atmosphere was funereal. The two presidents, and even the prime minister, recognised that hopes for a substantive summit were dead. Eisenhower suggested calling a full meeting for that afternoon. He expected that 'Mr Khrushchev probably would not come and the three Western heads of government could then make a joint declaration'. Macmillan agreed, adding that 'the important thing was to bring the conference to a conclusion in the proper way'. They should not allow Khrushchev to make another scene about 'the aircraft'. He suggested the invitation should say specifically that this was to be part of the full summit. De Gaulle agreed to write to the heads of government inviting them to attend at three o'clock. The two Western leaders would agree in writing to come. If Khrushchev refused, de Gaulle 'would then state that the summit conference could evidently not be held'.[77]

De Gaulle's declaration of support after the meeting with Khrushchev on 16 May had greatly heartened Eisenhower. Macmillan's behaviour had been less reassuring, culminating in his suggestion that the president apologise to Khrushchev. If the summit was to break up, Eisenhower now wanted to ensure that Macmillan would not distance himself from the events by blaming everything on the Americans. On leaving the Elysée after the morning meeting, he startled Macmillan by inviting the prime minister to ride with him in his open-top car. 'Ike's object was clear – ingeniously clear,' reflected Macmillan in his diary. 'If Khrushchev must break up the summit conference, there is no reason to let him break up the Anglo-American alliance.'[78] As the two leaders drove, de Gaulle dispatched letters to them and Khrushchev.[79] The Soviet premier was out enjoying himself in the French countryside at Pleur-sur-Marne when he received his invitation. He immediately drove back to Paris at full speed.

It all ended in farce. At three o'clock, Macmillan, Eisenhower and de Gaulle sat down in the Elysée Palace to wait for Khrushchev. De Gaulle noted that the Soviet premier had last been sighted in a 'barn in the country' giving a press conference.[80] Having sped back to Paris, the Soviet leader – ever the showman – announced that he was relaxing in his bath at the embassy.[81]

A few minutes before three o'clock, Koudriachef, counsellor at the Soviet embassy, telephoned the Elysée to ask the purpose of this meeting. If this was supposed to be part of the conference, Khrushchev would not come. If not, he would attend, but could not come until five as 'he was very tired and had not had any lunch'.[82] De Gaulle was furious. 'The situation was very clear', he fired back. It was now obvious that 'the summit meeting was unable to convene', he suggested to Macmillan and Eisenhower. The American agreed.[83]

For Eisenhower and de Gaulle, the summit was dead. Only the formalities remained. Soviet demands had been unacceptable and delivered in an insulting manner. The two presidents demanded that Khrushchev should be denounced. After his outrageous behaviour, Eisenhower hoped the Soviet leader would become '*persona non grata*'. Macmillan disagreed. Even now that Khrushchev had failed to attend the three o'clock meeting, the prime minister urged his colleagues to make one last effort for reconciliation:

> It would be a good idea if president de Gaulle would see him (Khrushchev), appeal to his sense of duty towards the world and beg him to take the view that his conditions had already been satisfied. It would probably not succeed but

the Western side must display the utmost patience. They could issue their declaration the following day after sleeping on the matter and after due deliberation.[84]

De Gaulle rejected this idea as ridiculous. 'Surely no one should tax the Western leaders with having displayed impatience', he demanded of Macmillan. 'Was it seriously contemplated that they should start an exercise of seduction all over again? Obviously it would not succeed.' Macmillan, who refused to accept de Gaulle's analysis, continued to urge delay. Without a formal reply from Khrushchev, they could not 'be in possession of the full picture'. If the Paris summit was to be 'the subject of debate for years to come', they must have written statement of positions. Moreover, it would be humiliating to end the summit with 'all of them hanging about in Paris together'. De Gaulle doubted that Khrushchev would bother to write. He would probably 'go on sending telephone messages and go on making trips into the country. [...] It might last a week,' he concluded in exasperation.[85]

Eisenhower wanted 'an early and dignified end'. But the president had known Macmillan for many years and, noticing the tears of frustration in his eyes, he whispered to Herter: 'You know, poor old Hal is very upset about this, and I think we might go as far as to meet him on this one point.'[86]

At half past three, Khrushchev sent another message from his bath. This inquired again whether the meeting was part of the summit or a discussion on the conditions that would enable the summit to begin. Eisenhower's views now hardened. He was 'getting fed up'. Khrushchev might be prepared to come and discuss conditions for a summit, but Eisenhower was not. 'Mr Khrushchev was acting like a dictator,' he said angrily. Notorious for his short temper and low boredom threshold, the president's patience had run out.[87]

As the meeting went on, Macmillan became increasingly distraught and his ideas more desperate. Could it not be, he asked the two presidents, that 'there might be some catch in the message as telephoned'? After all, that message had 'cleverly ... referred to the conditions and not to the Russian conditions'.

As Macmillan became increasingly hot under the collar, so de Gaulle turned glacial. Was it really Macmillan's suggestion, he icily inquired, that 'if this second message were not put into writing there would have to be a meeting with Mr Khrushchev to find out what it meant?' There was 'a limit to what he personally could do'. The facts were simple: Khrushchev had 'not turned up' and 'in these circumstances it had not been possible for the meeting to take place'.[88]

When another note arrived from Khrushchev saying he wanted an answer to his previous questions, exchanges between the three western leaders became hostile and terse. Eisenhower announced again that he was 'fed up and getting sick of the whole thing'. He 'didn't care' any more. Surely Khrushchev had a point, Macmillan inquired? Khrushchev had asked a question to which he had received no reply. That request should be 'answered in writing'. Eisenhower retorted that it was 'Khrushchev [who] had not answered president de Gaulle's invitation nor turned up at the meeting. [...] The fact that Mr Khrushchev has asked what kind of meeting it would be proved that he had no intention of coming to a real one.'[89]

De Gaulle supported Eisenhower and made it clear that he had taken enough from Khrushchev: 'He would not be party to writing any more letters to Mr Khrushchev. He [Khrushchev] had not answered his first one yet. The whole situation was very Byzantine.'[90] As if to emphasise the point, Khrushchev sent yet another message to clarify his intentions. De Gaulle announced that a Soviet press spokesman had told reporters that he was willing to participate in a summit 'as soon as President Eisenhower had expressed regret for what had happened, had condemned the policy of overflights and had undertaken to punish those responsible'.

'That settled it,' Macmillan later recalled. All he could do was urge delay on his partners. 'A great and tragic event had … occurred,' he told de Gaulle and Eisenhower: 'the policy for which [we] had all worked for two years had collapsed and the danger of war had loomed nearer'. They would issue no immediate communiqué. The Western leaders should meet the following day and 'only issue the communiqué if by then nothing new had developed'.[91]

Eisenhower and de Gaulle were unimpressed. De Gaulle 'could not see what new development of significance could be expected to occur before the following morning'. Eisenhower, his patience in shreds, chastised Macmillan for advocating a course of action that would end in 'confusion and embarrassment'. 'It was important to show unity at this juncture,' he observed testily.[92]

Unable to reach a resolution, the three leaders compromised by agreeing to meet again at half past nine that evening. As the meeting closed, they offered their own conclusions on events. Each was typical of the man. With his penchant for overblown and theatrical rhetoric, Macmillan noted that 'the collapse of the summit conference would be a bitter blow in his country. People had been praying in the churches for its success and now it had turned out to be a flop'. De Gaulle was more measured. The situation was not 'as bad as that'. He was 'sorry that the summit had not got going but there could be other conferences in the future'. Eisenhower was typically blunt: 'the way in which Mr Khrushchev had behaved that day showed what a scoundrel he was. The time had come to cut the tail off the cat.'[93]

Macmillan's attitude had caused considerable disquiet within the American delegation. Bohlen had urged Herter not to accept the prime minister's emotional appeal to give Khrushchev one last chance. As the 3pm meeting at the Elysée had progressed, so Eisenhower himself had become increasingly irritated with Macmillan. Back at the ambassador's residence, he put the PM's behaviour down to showmanship. Eisenhower told John Hay

Whitney that Macmillan's extraordinary behaviour had not bothered him. 'I know Harold well', the president said, 'and that's just an act he puts on'.[94] Philip de Zulueta thought otherwise. He recognised the very personal way in which Macmillan had taken this setback, reflecting later that 'I never saw him more depressed'.[95]

It was left to Selwyn Lloyd to contain the fall-out. At 6:45pm, Soviet foreign minister Gromyko came by invitation to the British embassy for talks with the foreign secretary. Where the previous day Macmillan had been cloying and sycophantic with Khrushchev, Lloyd was firm and business-like with Gromyko. After all, he pointed out, the two were now 'old friends or at least old colleagues'.[96] Lloyd's intention was clear. He wanted to take up the offer made by Khrushchev of reconvening the summit meeting in six to eight months time. They had to make sure that 'the dust should be allowed to settle'. Both sides had worked so hard for the 'relaxation of tension'. Lloyd hoped 'to pursue this common purpose together and meet again when the time was ripe'. In the meantime, it was important to 'keep tension low'.[97]

Khrushchev had always threatened that if the conference failed, he would sign a peace treaty with East Germany.[98] Therefore, it must have come as a relief to the British when Gromyko hinted that the Soviet Union would take no immediate action on Berlin. 'The Soviet government's policy was not an opportunist one,' the foreign minister told Lloyd. They would continue to follow 'a consistent policy of relaxation'. He suggested that 'it would be a very good thing if Her Majesty's government and other governments concerned acted similarly during the intervening period and if they and others did nothing which might prevent the lessening of international tension'. If 'certain quarters sought to increase tension and to heighten passions and throw fuel on the flames, then it could only worsen the prospects for a future summit meeting'.[99]

Gromyko's conversation with Lloyd restored a degree of equilibrium to East-West relations. Fears that Khrushchev would fly from Paris to Pankow in order to sign a peace treaty with East Germany now seemed unfounded. Thus, at 9:30pm, the three Western leaders came together to draw a curtain over the summit. It was a short, sombre and rather perfunctory meeting. Macmillan, feeling easier after Lloyd's talk with Gromyko, thought he 'could no longer ask for delay'.[100] As such, the foreign minister issued a communiqué at 10pm. It was terse and to the point:

> [The Western leaders] take note of the fact that because of the attitude adopted by the Chairman of the Council of Ministers of the Soviet Union it has not been possible to begin, at the summit conference, the examination of the problems which it had been agreed would be discussed between the four Chiefs of State or government. [...] They regret that these discussions, so important for world peace, could not take place. For their part, they remain unshaken in their conviction that all outstanding international questions should be settled not by the use or threat of force but by peaceful means through negotiation. They themselves remain ready to take part in such negotiations at any suitable time in the future.[101]

'So ended – before it had ever begun – the summit conference,' concluded Macmillan in his diary. There is no doubting his personal despair about the failure of the meeting. He had rested so many hopes on its success. Now the whole venture had ended in ignominious failure. Philip de Zulueta remembered that 'he was really cast down and glum after it'. Harold Evans, Macmillan's press secretary, recalled that for Macmillan, the summit was 'a moment of despair' and 'his first serious set-back since becoming prime minister'. As de Zulueta pointed out:

Apart from all the effort he had personally put into it, this was the moment he suddenly realised that Britain counted for nothing; he couldn't move Ike to make a gesture towards Khrushchev, and de Gaulle was simply not interested. I think this represented a real watershed in his life.[102]

Macmillan may have been in despair, but he did not neglect to attend to the political fall-out at home. 'I rang the Chief Whip and asked him if I should resign now my policy is in ruins around me,' he told Harold Evans on 19 May. 'He told me to hang on.' Macmillan went on that 'we ought to find a scapegoat. Perhaps we should make Selwyn resign.' The 'bleating' Lloyd, who overheard, was not amused.[103] Macmillan's one political consolation was that the press remained sympathetic. In the face of such a total collapse, the press evoked the spirit of 'Dunkirk'. 'Don't give up now, Mac!' read the unusually supportive banner headline of the *Daily Herald*. 'Khrushchev should have no illusions' the paper told its readers. 'Nobody had tried to bully us like he has since Hitler and Stalin. And the plain man's answer to him is: Go to Hell.'[104] The *Evening Standard* echoed these sentiments. The breakdown of the summit was 'a tragedy' but 'if the price of keeping the talks going is surrender to Mr K. then it is better that he should come home'. It was up to Britain and its allies to stand together with 'dignity, determination and unity'.[105] Nevertheless, there could be no disguising the sense of disappointment. It had been a 'bitter end' to a 'summit that never was' and the principal feeling was of bemusement.[106] 'At the end of a devastating week', commented the *Mail*, 'people are wondering [why...] the collapse of this summit has been so sudden, unexpected and even inexplicable'.[107] Could East and West ever 'work out some way of living together'?[108]

With the summit over, only the formalities of leave-taking remained. On the morning of 19 May, Khrushchev paid brief visits to Macmillan and de Gaulle to say his farewells. He did not attempt to see Eisenhower, whom he would never meet again. He told Macmillan that blame for the failure of the summit rested with 'the Pentagon and the reactionary forces' of the US, but thanked the prime minister for his 'efforts to bring about the summit conference and the personal contribution he had made to have it take place'. He also made a veiled threat that as the West was unwilling to resolve the Berlin question, he might be 'obliged to seek a unilateral solution'. Macmillan urged him to 'wait until the dust settled and let it settle quickly' rather than do anything precipitate. Each side should act 'in such a way as to make it possible for a new start to be made'.[109]

Macmillan may have been less civil had he known what had transpired the previous evening at the Soviet embassy. When it had come up in conversation that Macmillan must surely be dining at that very moment in his formal dinner jacket, Khrushchev instructed officials to run to the British embassy to summon the prime minister with the promise of a last minute compromise. 'Say that I want to talk with him here, that the only possible time is tonight, and that he must be here in forty-five minutes, no later,' Khrushchev drunkenly demanded. 'I want him to rush here, so that I can see him with omelette all over his dinner jacket.' Only Andrei Gromyko's intervention saved Macmillan the final indignity as the butt of a nasty practical joke.[110]

In the afternoon, the three Western leaders met to say their goodbyes. Despite their sense of disappointment, all three attempted to bring levity to the situation. They bantered about when to let in the photographers. Eisenhower suggested placing an empty chair between the leaders.[111] Yet for all his good humour, there was no disguising Eisenhower's sense of disappointment. The president was a practical man whose use of language, particularly the written word, was direct and unsentimental. He did not engage in the written declarations of affection that Macmillan so regularly employed. Yet there can be no mistaking the genuine sense of emotional strain in Eisenhower's letters and speeches in the days immediately after the summit.

Eisenhower's note to de Gaulle displayed genuine warmth and affection. The conference had been very stressful. De Gaulle had been supportive: Eisenhower was grateful.[112] In a glowing and effusive tribute, he told the French president:

> I leave Paris with the warmth and strength of your friend-ship, so amply demonstrated and renewed under the stress of the last four days, an even more valued possession than ever before. You and I have shared great experiences in war and in peace, and from those experiences has come, for my part at least, a respect and admiration that I have for few men. [...] Certainly the word 'ally' has for me now an even deeper meaning than ever before. I salute the staunch determination that you and your countrymen have shown.[113]

Writing to Macmillan, the president was less fulsome, but remained affectionate. Conscious of the need to keep up the prime minister's spirits, he told him that 'you did everything that you possibly could to bring about a degree of civilised behaviour in the arrogant and intransigent man from Moscow; no-one could have tried harder ... no-one could have done more'. The letter was signed, in his own hand, 'always, your devoted friend as ever, Ike'.[114]

Eisenhower had good cause to worry about Macmillan's low spirits. The prime minister did not attempt to hide his abject distress from friends and allies. To the Australian prime minister, Robert Menzies, he wrote:

> I cannot conceal from you that the result or rather the lack of it, has been a great disappointment to me. As you know I have for nearly two years now believed in and worked for a meeting between the heads of government of East and West to discuss the urgent problems which increase the tensions and difficulties in the world ... The road to the

summit has been long and difficult. There have been many ups and downs. Nevertheless I had hoped that we were at last really about to enter upon those serious negotiations which I believe to be so essential to the peace of the world.[115]

Macmillan left France on the afternoon of 19 May in physical and emotional agony. 'I felt very tired today, with much pain in the region of the heart', he wrote in his diary. 'Is it thrombosis or indigestion? I can scarcely do anything ..., either reading or writing.' Two days later, he spent the morning in bed writing up the events of Paris. His conclusion was bleak: 'The Summit – on which I had set high hopes and for which I worked for over 2 years – has blown up, like a volcano! It is ignominious; it is tragic; it is almost incredible'.[116]

'A horrid, cold, drizzly day,' Macmillan wrote miserably at the end of his account. 'Read *Dombey and Son* and slept during afternoon'.[117]

Epilogue

'King to king'

MACMILLAN'S SUMMIT POLICY was dead. He had worked for more than two years to secure a meeting of the leaders of the 'Great Powers'. When the conference at Paris imploded, Macmillan departed in humiliation. The *Herald Tribune* adroitly observed that the prime minister left the summit 'the most weakened, diplomatically, of any of the western big three leaders'.[1]

All hopes of a summit in the near or middle future plummeted. Selwyn Lloyd conducted a round of discussions with European ambassadors after Paris and conceded that 'we should have to wait at least until about this time next year' before thinking about another heads of government conference. Moreover, he added, it would be 'very difficult to convince the Americans of the desirability of another Summit meeting'.[2] Macmillan thought the prospects even bleaker. 'I fear that it must be doubtful if negotiations, at least at the level of heads of government, will really be possible even a year from now after the way President Eisenhower was treated, and negotiations later than May 1961 will inevitably be held under the shadow of the forthcoming German elections,' he told Lloyd. It was 'difficult for the moment to see our way ahead'.[3]

A meeting of the National Security Council on 24 May eliminated any doubt about the American position. Allies should know that any attempt to initiate another summit 'would be interpreted as a sign of weakness'.[4] Macmillan had concluded that

Britain might not 'usefully talk to the Americans for the next months'.[5] Now Eisenhower confirmed that summitry was off the agenda.

Macmillan had worked for more than eighteen months to achieve a summit. By May 1960, almost his entire foreign policy strategy was dependent on the success of the summitry, including the far-reaching 'Future Policy, 1960–1970.' At the heart of the report was 'the need to avoid an absolute choice between North America on the one hand and the continent of Europe on the other; that we should rather aim to bind together one comprehensive Atlantic community'.[6] Summitry was the practical way in which Macmillan had expected to fulfil that agenda. He had set out to establish a system, not unlike the nineteenth century Holy Alliance, whereby heads of government would meet at regular summits. This might enable Britain to retain its influence on the world stage, whilst relaxing its expensive global responsibilities. As Lloyd commented to Macmillan, Britain had 'a number of albatrosses' around its neck, but they could be 'disposed of without necessarily surrendering British interests. As we do so, we shall steadily grow stronger in influence'.[7]

Macmillan had taken a very personal lead in establishing the summit policy. Its rationale had depended on his ability to influence other leaders in face-to-face discussions. Therefore, it was personally galling to perform so badly at Paris in dealing with the most important friendship of all. Eisenhower clearly had certain affection for Harold Macmillan. The prime minister could be very amusing company. When Eisenhower visited London in August 1959, Macmillan took every trouble to make the visit a happy one. He pulled off so well the small touches, such as giving himself his wartime rank of political adviser for an official dinner, which allowed Eisenhower to seat himself between old comrades. When the president returned home, he wrote to Macmillan, with uncharacteristic emotion, that 'the unique and friendly character of this latest of our conferences ...

was engendered … by the close relationship between the two of us that seemingly grows stronger every time we meet'. The president enjoyed Macmillan fussing around him and responded well to his sentimental reminiscences about the old days. Macmillan's error was to exaggerate the extent to which he might exploit that genuine personal affection.[8]

Macmillan's misjudgement of Eisenhower at Paris was profound. When the president came to the summit, his credibility with American and world opinion was extremely low. The U–2 incident was a humiliation for him. By admitting to spying, the first president to do so publicly, he stood accused of destroying America's moral authority in the battle against communism. Moreover, the U–2 incident exposed Eisenhower to the charge of incompetence. It gave the impression of a president who did not run his own administration, and a defence establishment that acted outside executive control. As Eisenhower's predecessor, Harry Truman, commented, America had been made to look 'ridiculous'. Ike had wanted to be a great peacemaker as well as a warmaker. In the last eighteen months of his presidency, he had hoped to make the world a safer place in which to live. Khrushchev's visit to Camp David, the summit in Paris, and an historic presidential trip to Moscow were expected to provide a magnificent end to an outstanding life of public service. The U–2 incident destroyed those hopes. According to his secretary, this left Ike 'very depressed' and even considering resignation. He arrived in Paris shaken, angry and upset, very aware that the meeting would 'not be a Sunday school picnic'. What he needed, and expected, was the support of those he called 'my old friends'.[9]

Macmillan had always made a great deal of his 'extraordinary relationship' with Eisenhower, even commenting that 'I was a sort of son to Ike'. If the Paris summit was an occasion when the president might have welcomed some filial affection, he was disappointed and angered by Macmillan's tepid loyalty.[10] De Gaulle's attitude compounded this perception. In particular, the

French president's 'Whatever happens, *we are with you*' had 'really warmed [Eisenhower's] heart'. De Gaulle had been a thorn in the president's side for two years, but at a critical moment, he had offered unhesitating loyalty. The strength of Eisenhower's gratitude was apparent in the letter he sent after the summit confirming 'a respect and admiration that I have for few men'.[11]

The collapse of the Paris summit was not just a problem for British foreign policy: it had been a personal catastrophe for Macmillan. In a letter to the Queen, he commented dejectedly that 'we have fallen from the summit into the deep crevasse'.[12] Yet that sense of falling from the summit was precipitate. What Macmillan could not have foreseen in May 1960 was that within the year his relationship with Eisenhower's successor would breathe new life into the Atlantic alliance.

Young, bright and debonair, the new president, John F. Kennedy, was born both literally and metaphorically in a different century to Macmillan. During the first months after Kennedy's election, the prime minister became increasingly gloomy about the prospects of forming a decent relationship with the new president, and started 'feeling his age'. De Zulueta confirmed Macmillan's own instincts by telling him in February 1961 that 'with President Eisenhower the appeal to sentiment and comradeship was more effective than intellectual argument. Clearly this will not be the case with Mr Kennedy'. The private secretary's conclusion that 'cosy chats ... will not impress Mr Kennedy or help to get better relations with him' was a disheartening one for the prime minister. Macmillan had always attached importance to personal friendships as a diplomatic weapon. In early 1961, it seemed that he needed 'somehow to convince him [JFK] that I am worth consulting not as an old friend ... but as a man who, although of advancing years, has young and fresh thoughts'. He could not have anticipated that, in fact, it would be his demeanour as the 'old campaigner' that would provide the basis for closest relationship of his premiership.[13]

The two leaders met for the first time at Key West, Florida and in Washington in the spring of 1961. Macmillan was impressed with the president from the outset. He was 'courteous, quiet, quick, decisive – and tough', as well as having 'something very eighteenth century' about him, which Macmillan found highly endearing. Yet Kennedy's classical charms could not hide the fact that he seemed uninterested in starting a 'special' relationship.[14]

The turning point came by courtesy of Khrushchev. The Russian leader's strong-arm tactics shocked Kennedy when they met in Vienna in June 1961. ('Politics is 'a merciless business', the Russian later said about the meeting.) The journey to Britain from Vienna, commented Kennedy's air force aide, was 'like riding with the losing baseball team after the World Series'. Arriving in London, Kennedy was angry and in low spirits, made worse by chronic back pain. At their first full meeting, Macmillan, sensing that JFK was fed-up, gave a nonchalant flick of the hand and said: 'Mr President, you have had a tiring day, don't let's have this … Why not come up to my room and we will have a little chat?' Kennedy seemed relieved by the suggestion and the two men sat consuming whisky and sandwiches for a few hours. It was exactly this kind of elegant casualness that so endeared Macmillan to Kennedy. Arthur Schlesinger, presidential aide and later Kennedy's official biographer, later commented on the 'considerable temperamental rapport' that the two leaders discovered at that meeting:

> Kennedy, with his own fondness for the British political style, liked Macmillan's patrician approach to politics, his impatience with official ritual, his insouciance with professionals, his pose of nonchalance, even when most deeply committed. Macmillan, for his part, responded to Kennedy's courage, his ability to see events unfolding against the vast canvas of history, his contempt for cliché,

his unfailing sense of the ridiculous. They found the same things funny and the same things serious. [...] They soon discovered that they could match each other's transitions from gravity to mischief and communicate in shorthand. It was as if they had known each other for life.[15]

During the next two and a half years, the personal relationship between Macmillan and Kennedy blossomed into friendship – a friendship that was kept well oiled by the British ambassador in Washington, David Ormbsy-Gore, an old friend of the president, whom he trusted 'as I would my own cabinet'. After JFK's assassination in November 1963, Macmillan felt the death like 'a personal bereavement'. Over the years, he exchanged long letters with the president's widow. 'People will say, "Do you remember those days – how perfect they were?" The days of you and Jack', she fondly told him.[16]

The warm, personal relationship between JFK and Macmillan would translate into special influence for Britain. During the Cuban missile crisis, the British ambassador contributed to meetings of the National Security Council, making a critical suggestion about the 'quarantine line'.[17] On a number of other important issues, Kennedy remained accommodating to Macmillan's political needs and personal ambitions. The president tried to bolster Macmillan's position during the Profumo crisis by flying to Birch Grove for personal talks despite opposition from aides and American newspapers. On the peace question, an issue that the president had planned to address after the 1963 election, he responded to Macmillan's cajoling by agreeing to a partial test ban treaty with the Soviets. 'So was realised at least one of the great purposes which I had set myself,' Macmillan later recorded.

Yet Macmillan's greatest realisation of personal diplomacy came during the Skybolt crisis. When the Americans finally admitted that the Skybolt missile system did not work, Macmillan insisted at a one-to-one meeting with the president at Nassau that Britain must have the opportunity to buy Polaris instead. Kennedy, belatedly aware that the issue was 'political dynamite' for Macmillan, scotched the objections of his own officials and gave the prime minister what he wanted. As Richard Neustadt has commented, 'it was a case of "king to king", and it infuriated the court'.[18]

Macmillan's relationship with JFK fulfilled at last his long-held expectations for personal diplomacy. Two decades earlier, he had watched with awe at Casablanca as Churchill sat in conference with Roosevelt. Churchill, with his sweeping vision and grand gestures, was the man above all others whom Macmillan wished to emulate. When he became prime minister in 1957, he resolved to conduct diplomacy in a Churchillian fashion, which meant personal talks at the highest level. He undertook the climb to the summit with a determination bordering on the obsessive. It was a personal initiative taken in the face of cabinet and Whitehall suspicions, exploiting temporary political and institutional weakness to brush aside objections.

Macmillan had not been afraid to use foreign policy initiatives to satisfy a domestic agenda. Certainly in 1959 he was more than happy to use the visit to Moscow to revive Conservative election hopes. Victory at the polls seven months later seemed to vindicate the strategy. Macmillan's conduct of personal diplomacy could sometimes appear seriously flawed. The Moscow visit, for example, alienated the French and Germans. Similarly, Macmillan's personal deal with Kennedy on Polaris gave de Gaulle just the excuse he needed to justify vetoing the British application to join the EEC, which delayed entry for another decade.

Yet Macmillan's summitry was at the centre of a genuine attempt to construct an overall strategy for Britain on the world stage. Like Churchill, Macmillan loved drawing up blueprints, such as 'Future Policy' and the 'Grand Design,' for a long-term British future. At the heart of all these plans was a prime minister's role on the international stage. Macmillan had a strong faith in his own ability to influence other heads of government, but on occasion, he was not very good at doing so. Adenauer clearly disliked him, a feeling that the prime minister reciprocated. Relations with de Gaulle were always courteous, but despite Macmillan's constant reminders about the 'old days', the French president always believed Macmillan to be too pro-American. Even Eisenhower, with whom Macmillan enjoyed a genuinely cordial relationship, often found him too cloying in his appeals to friendship.

Finally, with Kennedy, Harold Macmillan shared a genuine friendship that had dramatic consequences for Britain. Kennedy bestowed favours to help him out of political fixes. Macmillan responded with unfailing public support and sympathetic private hearings. Part of the reason for the relationship's success was that both leaders understood their place. The lesson of the Paris summit for Macmillan was that 'Britain counted for nothing'. Therefore when he approached the new president, it was no longer as emperor to emperor (as with Churchill to Roosevelt), but more as powerful baron to king. Offering his counsel and influence in this way, Macmillan endeared himself to Kennedy, who enjoyed his friendship, trusted his loyalty, and respected his experience of international affairs.

Jacqueline Kennedy got to the heart of this when she wrote to Macmillan after her husband's death that JFK had thought of him as 'almost an equal'. It was not the epitaph that Macmillan would have wanted when he took office in 1957. By 1963, he recognised it as a position that would enable Britain to carry on punching above its weight in world affairs. Keeping close to a friend had obvious advantages when that friend was the world's no.1 power.[19]

Notes

CHAPTER ONE

1 J. Scarisbrick, *Henry VIII* (London, 1981), pp 74–9.

2 J. Young [ed.], *The foreign policy of Churchill's peacetime administration, 1951–55* (Leicester, 1988), p. 55.

3 See D. Reynolds, *In command of history: Churchill fighting and writing the second world war* (London, 2004).

4 M. Gilbert, Winston S. Churchill: vol. 8, *Never despair* (London, 1988), pp 509–10.

5 On this topic, see K. Larres, *Churchill's cold war: the politics of personal diplomacy* (New Haven and London, 2002).

6 Young, *Churchill's peacetime administration*, pp 55–7 (quotation, p. 56).

7 Ibid., pp 75–7.

8 Ibid., p. 15.

9 For an outline of these proposals, see: S. Ambrose, *Eisenhower: the president* (New York, 1984), pp 263–5.

10 R. Rhodes James, *Anthony Eden* (London, 1986), p. 417.

11 Sanders, *Losing an empire*, p. 72.

12 Historian and journalist, Keith Kyle was working for *The Economist* in Washington at this time. He recalls that, when news came through about the British and French ultimatum to Egypt and Israel, 'like most people in Washington, I never for a moment supposed ... that what I saw could be taken at face value or could be anything other than some form of collusion between Britain, France and Israel': K. Kyle, *Suez* (London, 1991), p. 1. In addition to Kyle's compelling narrative study, see: W. Louis & R. Owen, *Suez, 1956: the crisis and its consequences* (Oxford, 1989); W.S. Lucas, *Divided we stand: Britain, the US and the Suez crisis* (London, 1991). For a more favourable assessment of Eden's role, see D.R. Thorpe, *Anthony Eden* (London, 2003).

13 Reynolds, *Britannia overruled* (London, 1991) p. 203.

14 Ibid., p. 205; Morgan, *People's peace*, pp 154–5.

15 P. Catterall, *The Macmillan diaries: the cabinet years, 1950–1957* (London, 2003), p. 616.

16 Macmillan is well served by his biographers, not least Alistair Horne, *Macmillan* (2 vols, London, 1988–9), and Simon Ball, *The guardsmen: Harold Macmillan, three friends and the world they made* (London, 2004).

17 P. Clarke, *A question of leadership: from Gladstone to Thatcher* (London, 1992), pp 211–12; R. Davenport-Hines, *The Macmillans* (London, 1992), p. 138; P. Gay, *Freud for historians* (Oxford, 1985), pp 94–6.

18 D. Healey, *The time of my life* (London, 1990), p. 192, although as James Barber points out: 'Macmillan, who was at first has been billed as "Supermac" partly from his confident handling of the media, later fell foul of the satire of the early 1960s when … [his] image was transformed from an unflappable leader to an incompetent old bumbler': Barber, *The prime minister since 1945* (Oxford, 1991), p. 39; see, for example, 'TV PM' from *Beyond the Fringe*, in F. Muir & S. Brett, *The Penguin book of comedy sketches* (London, 1992), pp 181–3.

19 Davenport-Hines, *The Macmillans*, p. 140.

20 Clarke, *A question of leadership*, pp 212–13; Davenport-Hines, *The Macmillans*, pp 163–4.

21 An example of Macmillan's less than dapper 'look' can be found in the photograph facing p. 139 in A. Horne, *Macmillan, volume 2, 1957–1986* (London, 1989).

22 R. Rhodes James, *Bob Boothby* (London, 1991), pp 112–13; P. Clarke, *A question of leadership*, p. 213; Davenport-Hines, *The Macmillans*, pp 175–6; The Cavendish family found Macmillan so boring that the women drew straws to see who had to suffer the tedium of sitting next to him at dinner.

23 Rhodes James, *Bob Boothby*, p. 113.

24 Horne, *Macmillan, volume 2*, p. 611.

25 A. Horne, *Macmillan, volume 1, 1894–1956* (London, 1988), p. 89; Clarke, *A question of leadership*, p. 211.

26 Clarke, *A question of leadership*, pp 215–16.

27 H. Macmillan, *War diaries: politics and war in the Mediterranean, January 1943–May 1945* (London, 1984), p. 8.

28 Horne, *Macmillan, volume 2*, p. 610.

29 *The Economist*, 13 February 1954.

30 Morgan, *People's peace*, pp 117–18.

31 Clarke, *Question of leadership*, p. 219.

32 Horne, *Macmillan, volume 1*, pp 367–79.

33 A. Shlaim, P. Jones & K. Sainsbury, *British foreign secretaries since 1945* (Newton Abbot, 1977), p. 110.

34 Clarke, *Question of leadership*, pp 221–2. On Macmillan's role in the Suez crisis, see Nigel Ashton, *Macmillan, Eisenhower and the problems of Nasser* (Basingstoke, 1996) and Peter Catterall's penetrating note in *The Macmillan diaries*, p. 607.

35 Horne, *Macmillan, volume 1*, p. 449.

36 Clarke, *Question of leadership*, p. 223.

37 Davenport-Hines, *The Macmillans*, p. 266.

38 R. Blake, *The Conservative party from Peel to Thatcher* (London, 1985), pp 278–81; Horne, *Macmillan, volume 2*, p. 8; Young, *Churchill's peacetime administration*, p. 68.

39 Blake, *The Conservative party*, p. 281.

40 V. Bogdanor & R. Skidelsky, *The age of affluence, 1951–64* (London, 1970), pp 17–18; N. Annan, *Our age: the generation that made post-war Britain* (London, 1991) pp 547–8.

41 Holland, *Pursuit of greatness*, pp 245, 279.

42 Catterall, *The Macmillan diaries*, p. 616.

CHAPTER TWO

1 *Daily Herald*, 9 January 1959, p. 1.

2 H. Macmillan, *Riding the storm, 1956–59* (London, 1971), p. 559.

3 R. Worcester, *British public opinion: a guide to the history and methodology of political opinion polling* (Oxford, 1991), pp 16–18.

4 State Dept. Tel 4544 from London, 3 February 1958; State Dept. Tel 4571 from London, 4 February 1958: National Archives of the United States, College Park, MD (henceforth NA (College Park)), State Dept. Decimal File 1955–59, RG59 611.61.

5 J. Goldblat and D. Cox (eds), *Nuclear weapons tests: prohibition or limitation* (Oxford, 1988), p. 3; America exploded the first H-bomb in 1952 and was followed by the USSR in 1953.

6 I. Clark & N. Wheeler, *The British origins of nuclear strategy, 1945–55* (Oxford, 1989), pp 210–11, 236–7.

7 D. Reynolds, *Britannia overruled* (London, 1991), p. 181.

8 R. Taylor, *Against the bomb: the British peace movement, 1958–65* (Oxford, 1988), pp 26–7.

9 Foreign Service Despatch 2323 from London, 30 December 1957: NA (College Park), State Department Decimal File 1955–59, RG59 611.11.

10 A. Horne, *Macmillan, volume 2, 1957–1986* (London, 1989), p. 116. Horne notes this comment was made at the end of Macmillan's first year of office, but then gives a reference date of February 1957. In view of Macmillan's attitude in February 1958, I am taking Horne's reference date to be correct.

11 H. Macmillan, *Riding the storm, 1956–59*, p. 460.

12 Symon to Bishop, 16 January 1959: The National Archives of the United Kingdom (TNA): Public Record Office (PRO), PREM11/2775.

13 Symon to Bishop, 16 January 1959: TNA, PRO, PREM11/2775; *Daily Express*, 19 December 1957, p. 1.

14 Macmillan to Lloyd, 28 January 1957: TNA, PRO, PREM11/2775; Record of conversation between the prime minister and Soviet ambassador, 4 February 1957: TNA, PRO, PREM11/2775

15 Macmillan made these points to Adenauer in May 1957. Record of prime minister's meeting with Dr Adenauer, 8 May 1957: TNA, PRO, PREM11/2775.

16 State Dept. tel. 3953 from London, 6 January 1958; State Dept. tel. 3940 from London, 5 January 1958: NA (College Park), State Department Decimal File 1955–59, RG59 741.13.

17 State Dept. to CIRCR, 6 January 1958; State Department tel. 4097 from London, 13 January 1958: NA (College Park), State Dept. Decimal File 1955–59, RG59 741.13.

18 Memorandum by the secretary of state for Foreign Affairs, 'Relations with the Soviet Union', 21 January 1958: TNA, PRO, CAB 129/91, C(58)9.

19 Ibid.

20 R. Blake, *The Conservative party from Peel to Thatcher* (London, 1985), p. 281.

21 State Dept. tel. 4544 from London, 3 February 1959: NA (College Park), State Dept. Decimal File 1955–59, RG59 741.13.

22 A. Sampson, *Macmillan: a study in ambiguity* (London, 1967), p. 142.

23 Lord Gladwyn, *The memoirs of Lord Gladwyn*, (London 1972), p. 277.

24 Cabinet meeting, 22 January 1958: TNA, PRO, CAB 128/32 CC(58), 8th conclusions, minute 4

25 Ironically, when Macmillan actually went to Moscow, Selwyn Lloyd would claim the idea for a visit to be his in the first place: D.R.Thorpe, *Selwyn Lloyd* (London, 1989), pp 287 & 297.

26 K. Kyle, *Suez* (London, 1991), pp 42 & 85–7.

27 Foreign Service Despatch 2934 from London, 28 February 1958: NA (College Park), State Department Decimal File 1955–59, RG59 741.13.

28 *Evening Standard*, 22 January 1959, p. 5.

29 Ibid., p. 4.

30 Macmillan, *Riding the storm*, p. 760.

31 Ibid., pp 760–1.

32 *The Times*, 24 February 1958.

33 State Dept. tel. 4321 from London 23 January 1958: NA (College Park), State Dept. Decimal File 1955–59, RG59 611.61.

34 State Dept. tel. 4363 from London, 24 January 1958: NA (College Park), State Dept. Decimal File 1955–59, RG59 611.61.

35 Foreign Service Despatch 2703 from London, 7 February 1958: NA (College Park), State Dept. Decimal File 1955–59, RG59 741.13.

36 State Dept. tel. 4386 from London, 25 January 1958: NA (College Park), State Dept. Decimal File 1955–59, RG59 611.61.

37 State Dept. tel. 4487 from London, 30 January 1958: NA (College Park), State Dept. Decimal File 1955–59, RG59 611.61.

38 When Butler met Soviet ambassador Malik on 30 January, the ambassador was strongly anti-American whilst emphasising Soviet willingness to sign a non-aggression pact ('a subject which we now find rather embarrassing', one foreign office official pointed out to the American embassy). State Dept. tel. 4488 from London, 30 January 1958: NA (College Park), State Dept. Decimal File 1955–59, RG59 611.61.

39 Foreign Service Despatch 2703 from London, 7 February 1958: NA (College Park), State Dept. Decimal File 1955–59, RG59 741.13.

40 For a full assessment of the policy of the Eisenhower administration on the question of summitry, see the elegant study by E. Bruce Geelhoed and Anthony O. Edmonds, *Eisenhower, Macmillan and allied unity, 1957–61* (Basingstoke, 2003).

41 See J. Gaddis, *Strategies of containment* (Oxford, 1982), pp 127–63.

42 J. Dougherty & R. Pfaltzgraff, *American foreign policy: FDR to Reagan* (New York, 1986), pp 95, 101–5.

43   S. Ambrose, *Eisenhower: the president* (New York, 1984), p. 445.
44   Pre-press conference briefing, 5 March 1958: Eisenhower Library (Abilene), Ann Whitman File, DDE Series, Box 31, Staff Notes, March 1958 (2).
45   State Dept. tel. 587 to Frankfurt, 24 January 1958: NA (College Park), State Dept. Decimal File 1955–59, RG59 611.61.
46   Goldblat and Cox (eds), *Nuclear weapons tests*, pp 8–9.
47   Conversation with Lloyd, London, 19 October 1958: Eisenhower Library (Abilene), Dulles Papers, General Correspondence Box 1, Memoranda of Conversations (General) L-M(1).
48   Macmillan, *Riding the storm*, p. 559.
49   For a full account of the Berlin crisis, see J. Schick, *The Berlin crisis, 1958–62* (Philadelphia, 1971), pp 3–133. A summary of the background and immediate events as seen by the foreign office at this time can be found in *Germany and European security*: TNA, PRO, FO 371/145820.
50   A. Gromyko & B. Ponomarev (eds), *Soviet foreign policy, volume 2, 1945–80* (Moscow, 1980), p. 297; Department of State translation of Soviet Note, 27 November 1958: Eisenhower Library (Abilene), Whitman File, Dulles/Herter series 8, Dulles, November 1958.
51   C. Keble, *Britain and the Soviet Union, 1917–89* (London, 1990), p. 258.
52   S. Talbott (ed.), *Khrushchev remembers* (London, 1971), p. 453.
53   Keble, *Britain and the Soviet Union*, p. 259.
54   386th Meeting of the NSC, 13 November 1958: Eisenhower Library (Abilene), Whitman File, NSC Series.
55   Ibid.
56   Telephone conversation with Dulles, 27 November 1958: Eisenhower Library (Abilene), Whitman File, DDE Diaries, Telephone Calls, November 1958.
57   Telephone call from president, 12 January 1959: Eisenhower Library (Abilene) Dulles Papers, Telephone Calls, Series 13, Memoranda of Telephone Conversations with White House, January-April 1959.
58   On the impact of the Berlin crisis on British policy, see John P.S. Gearson, *Harold Macmillan and the Berlin wall crisis, 1958–62: the limits of interest and force* (Basingstoke, 1998) and Sabine Lee, *An uneasy partnership: British-German relations, 1955–61* (Bochum, 1996).
59   *The Times*, 28 November 1958, p. 11.
60   *The Times*, 4 December 1958, p. 13; 13 December 1958, p. 7.
61   *Daily Mail*, 28 October 1958, p. 1.
62   'Relations with the Soviet Union', 21 January 1958: TNA, PRO, CAB 29/91, C(58)9
63   Telephone conversation with Dulles, 20 January 1959: Eisenhower Library (Abilene) Whitman File, DDE Diary 38, Telephone Calls, January 1959; Telephone conversation with president, 20 January 1959: Eisenhower Library (Abilene), Dulles Papers, Telephone Calls, Series 13, Memoranda of Telephone Calls – White House, January-April 1959.
64   Telephone conversation with Dulles, 20 January 1959: Eisenhower Library (Abilene) Whitman File, DDE Diary 38, Telephone Calls, January 1959: Telephone conversation with president, 20 January 1959: Eisenhower Library

(Abilene), Dulles Papers, Telephone Calls, Series 13, Memoranda of Telephone Calls – White House, January-April 1959.

65   Memorandum of Private Conversation with Sir Harold Caccia, 21 January 1959: Eisenhower Library (Abilene) Dulles Papers, Subject Series 11, Macmillan/Lloyd Correspondence, 1959,

66   Telephone call from the secretary of state, 21 January 1959: Eisenhower Library (Abilene) Whitman File, DDE Diary 38, Telephone Calls, January 1959.

67   Foreign office tel. 414 to Washington, 20 January 1959 (Talking paper from prime minister for Caccia to use with Dulles): TNA, PRO, PREM11/2775.

68   Telephone call with president, 21 January 1959: Eisenhower Library (Abilene), Dulles Papers, Telephone Calls Series 13, Memoranda of Telephone Calls – White House, January–April 1959.

69   Memorandum of private conversation with Sir Harold Caccia, 21 January 1959: Eisenhower Library (Abilene) Dulles Papers, Subject Series 11, Macmillan/Lloyd Correspondence, 1959

70   Macmillan, *Riding the storm*, pp 583–7.

71   Macmillan to secretary of state for Commonwealth Relations, 3 February 1959: TNA, PRO, FO 371/143433. Macmillan informed Home that the Soviets had accepted his proposal and commented: 'I trust you feel that it is right to have taken this initiative.'

72   Cabinet meeting, 3 February 1959: TNA, PRO, CAB 128/33, CC(59), 4th Conclusions, Minute 1.

73   J. Young (ed.), *The foreign policy of Churchill's peacetime administration, 1951–1955* (Leicester, 1988), p. 56.

74   CC(59), 4th Conclusions, Minute 1: TNA, PRO, CAB 128/33; Blake, *The Conservative party from Peel to Thatcher*, pp 279–81.

75   J. Lacouture, *De Gaulle: the ruler, 1945–70* (London, 1991), pp 334–8.

76   See Sabine Lee, *An uneasy partnership: British-German relations, 1955–61* (Bochum, 1996). Horne, *Macmillan, volume 2*, pp 134–5; *Frankfurter Allgemeine Zeitung*, 2 April 1958.

77   Keble, *Britain and the Soviet Union*, p. 256 The letter also proposed substantial disarmament and a test ban, a slightly embarrassing proposal given that Britain was set to begin its thermo-nuclear testing the following month.

78   Keble, *Britain and the Soviet Union*, pp 257–8.

79   Moscow tel. 136 to foreign office, 29 January 1959: TNA, PRO, FO 371/143433.

80   Moscow tel. 123 to foreign office, 27 January 1959: TNA, PRO, FO 371/143433.

81   Prime minister's Statement to the House of Commons, 5 February 1959: TNA, PRO, FO 371/143433.

82   Horne, *Macmillan, volume 2*, p. 122.

83   *Daily Mail*, 4 February 1959, p. 1.

84   *The Times*, 5 February 1959.

85   *Evening Standard*, 5 February 1959, p. 5.

86   *Daily Herald*, 6 February 1959, p. 1.

87 Moscow tel. 171 to foreign office, 4 February 1959: TNA, PRO, PREM11/2690.

88 Foreign office minute, 3 February 1959; TNA, PRO, FO 371/135350.

89 Brook to prime minister, 18 February 1959: *Steering brief for prime minister's visit to Moscow*, 2 February 1959: TNA, PRO PREM11/2690 & FO 371/143686; *Brief for the prime minister's visit to Moscow*, Report by the Joint Planning Staff of the Chiefs of Staff Committee, 9 February 1959: TNA, PRO, DEFE 4/116, JP(59)17(final).

90 Lee, *An uneasy partnership: British-German relations*. Full text of the Jebb memorandum is published as an appendix.

91 Foreign Service Despatch 1912 from London: National Archives of the United States (Washington D.C.), State Department Decimal File 1955–59, RG59, 741.13.

92 Lee, *An uneasy partnership: British-German relations;* Top Secret Annex to Visit of the prime minister and foreign secretary to the Soviet Union, 21 February–3 March 1959: TNA, PRO, CAB 133/293.

93 Foreign office Minute from P.F. Hancock, 14 February 1959: TNA, PRO, FO 371/145819.

94 Ibid.

95 Ibid.

96 Noted in Brook to prime minister, 18 February 1959: TNA, PRO, PREM11/2690.

97 Brook to prime minister, 18 February 1959: TNA, PRO, PREM11/2690.

98 A full record of Macmillan's itinerary can be found in the foreword to 'Visit of the prime minister and foreign secretary to the Soviet Union, 21 February–3 March 1959': TNA, PRO, CAB 133/293.

99 Macmillan diary, 6 January 1959. Peter Catterall, *The Macmillan diaries, volume 2* (London, forthcoming).

100 H. Evans, *Downing Street diary: the Macmillan years, 1957–63* (London, 1981), p. 75.

101 *Daily Mail*, 22 February 1959, p. 1. Macmillan would have been amused to learn that he had started something of a fashion in London. As the *Daily Mail* informed readers: 'If-you-want-to-get-ahead note: a copy of Mr Macmillan's hat will set a new style at the men's wear fair at Earl's Court.' A male model will also wear a copy of the Premier's wide collared suit. The new fashion will be called the "British PM look".'

102 *Daily Mail*, 21–2 February 1959, p. 1; similar comments in *The Times*, 23 February 1959, p. 8; *Evening Standard*, 21 February 1959, p. 1.

103 *Daily Herald*, 21 February 1959, p. 1.

104 *The Times*, 23 February 1959, p. 8.

105 Evans, *Downing Street diary*, p. 75.

106 Macmillan, *Riding the storm*, p. 594.

107 'Visit of the prime minister and foreign secretary to the Soviet Union, 21 February–3 March 1959': TNA, PRO, CAB 133/293, p. 9. (This single bound volume collects all the records of conversations held during the Moscow visit and is used extensively in the narrative.)

108　Evans, *Downing Street diary*, p. 75. Catterall, *The Macmillan diaries, volume 2*.
109　Horne, *Macmillan, volume 2*, p. 124.
110　'Visit of prime minister to Soviet Union': TNA, PRO, CAB 133/293, *foreword*
111　Macmillan, *Riding the storm*, p. 598.
112　'Visit of prime minister to Soviet Union': TNA, PRO, CAB 133/293, pp 10–14.
113　Moscow tel. 330 to foreign office, 22 February 1959: TNA, PRO, PREM11/
　　　2690.
114　Moscow tel. 336 to foreign office, 23 February 1959: TNA, PRO, PREM11/
　　　2690.
115　'Visit of prime minister to Soviet Union': TNA, PRO, CAB 133/293.
116　Macmillan to Adenauer, Moscow tel. 332 to foreign office, 23 February
　　　1959: TNA, PRO, PREM11/2690.
117　Ibid.
118　Ibid.
119　*Evening Standard*, 24 February 1959, p. 5.
120　Macmillan, *Riding the storm*, p. 604.
121　*Daily Mail*, 24 February 1959, p. 8.
122　Sampson, *Macmillan*, p. 145.
123　Macmillan, *Riding the storm*, pp 606–7; *Daily Mail*, 25 February 1959, p. 1.
124　Macmillan, *Riding the storm*, p. 607.
125　Washington tel. 532 to foreign office, 25 February 1959: TNA, PRO, FO
　　　371/143437; Paris tel. 70 to foreign office, 25 February 1959: TNA, PRO,
　　　FO 371/143437; State Dept. tel. 3090 from London, 25 February 1959: NA
　　　(College Park), State Dept. Decimal File, 1955–59, RG59, 611.61.
126　*Daily Herald*, 25 February 1959, p. 1.
127　*The Times*, 25 February 1959, p. 10.
128　Macmillan, *Riding the storm*, p. 608.
129　Ibid.
130　On Khrushchev's contradictory nature, see most persuasively William
　　　Taubman, *Khrushchev: the man and his era* (New York, 2002). For a literary
　　　example of how this kind of body language can be used, the reader may care
　　　to see: I. McEwan, *The comfort of strangers* (London, 1981), p. 73.
131　*Visit of prime minister to Soviet Union*, pp 29–33: TNA, PRO, CAB 133/293.
132　Ibid.
133　Horne, *Macmillan, volume 2*, p. 125.
134　'Visit of prime minister to Soviet Union', pp 29–33: TNA, PRO, CAB
　　　133/293; Horne, *Macmillan, volume 2*, p. 125.
135　*Daily Mail*, 26 February 1959, p. 6.
136　'Visit of prime minister to Soviet Union', pp 36–7: TNA, PRO, CAB 133/293.
137　Macmillan, *Riding the storm*, p. 617.
138　'Visit of prime minister to Soviet Union', pp 36–7: TNA, PRO, CAB 133/293.
139　Dean to Hoyer Millar, Moscow tel. 374 to foreign office, 26 February 1959:
　　　TNA, PRO, PREM11/2690.
140　'Visit of prime minister to Soviet Union', p. 36–7: TNA, PRO, CAB 133/293;
　　　Daily Review of Soviet press (Soviet Information Bureau) 28 February 1959:
　　　TNA, PRO, FO 371/143440.

141 Taubman, *Khrushchev*, p. 412

142 Macmillan, *Riding the storm*, p. 618; recollection of Lord Brimelow, who (as Thomas Brimelow) travelled to Moscow with Macmillan: Sabine Lee, *An uneasy partnership: British-German relations, 1955–61* (Bochum, 1996).

143 Evans, *Downing Street diary*, p. 76. Evans account of the British line is confirmed in Moscow tel. 378 to foreign office, 26 February 1959: TNA, PRO, PREM11/2690.

144 Sampson, *Macmillan*, p. 146.

145 *Evening Standard*, 27 February 1959, p. 12.

146 *Daily Mail*, 27 February 1959, p. 1.

147 *The Times*, 27 February 1959, p. 8.

148 *Daily Herald*, 26–27 February 1959, p. 1.

149 Sampson, *Macmillan*, p. 146.

150 Washington tel. 532 to foreign office, 26 February 1959: TNA, PRO, PREM11/2690.

151 Telephone call from president to Herter, 24 February 1959: Eisenhower Library (Abilene), Herter papers 10, presidential Calls, 1959(2).

152 Livingston Merchant, Memorandum for the Record, 26 February 1959: NA (College Park), State Dept. Decimal File 1955–59, RG59, 611.61.

153 De Gaulle to Macmillan, Paris tel. 73 to foreign office, 27 February 1959: TNA, PRO, PREM11/2690.

154 Macmillan to Eisenhower, Moscow tel. 365 to foreign office, 26 February 1959: Macmillan to de Gaulle, Moscow tel. 336 to foreign office, 26 February 1959: TNA, PRO, PREM11/2690.

155 Macmillan, *Riding the storm*, p. 622.

156 Top Secret annex to 'Visit of prime minister to Soviet Union': TNA, PRO, CAB 133/293.

157 Moscow tel. 403 to foreign office, 1 March 1959: TNA, PRO PREM11/2690.

158 Macmillan to Eisenhower, Moscow tel. 409 to foreign office, 2 March 1959: Macmillan to de Gaulle (and Adenauer), Moscow tel. 408 to foreign office, 2 March 1959: TNA, PRO, PREM11/2690.

159 State Dept. tel. 3090 from Paris, 26 February 1959: NA (College Park), State Dept. Decimal File 1955–59, RG59, 611.61.

160 Ibid.

161 Telephone call to president, 2 March 1959: Eisenhower Library (Abilene), Herter Papers 10, presidential calls, 1959 (2).

162 Memorandum by the Chief of Naval Operations for the JCS on Berlin, 4 March 1959, JCS 1907/169: NA (College Park), Twining Papers, RG134, Berlin 1959.

163 Special meeting of the National Security Council, 5 March 1959: Eisenhower Library (Abilene), Whitman File, NSC Series 11.

164 'Visit of prime minister to Soviet Union': TNA, PRO, CAB 133/293, pp 38–42.

165 State Dept. to CIRCR, 6 January 1958: NA (College Park), State Dept. Decimal File 1955–59, RG59 741.13.

166 'Visit of prime minister to Soviet Union': TNA, PRO, CAB 133/293, pp 38–42.

167 Moscow tel. 422 to foreign office, 3 March 1959: TNA, PRO, PREM11/2685.

168 Macmillan, *Riding the storm*, pp 626–7.

169 Evans, *Downing Street diary*, p. 76.

170 B. Bruce, *Images of power: how the image makers shape our leaders* (London, 1992), p. 31.

171 *Daily Mail*, 3 March 1959, p. 1.

172 Moscow tel. 396 to foreign office, 28 February 1959: TNA, PRO, FO 371/143437; Moscow tel. 435 to foreign office, 3 March 1959: TNA, PRO, FO 371/143437.

173 Daily Review of Soviet press (Soviet Information Bureau), 4 March 1959: TNA, PRO, FO 371/143440.

174 e.g. *The Times*, 4 March 1959, p. 8.

175 *The Times*, 4 March 1959, p. 8.

176 *Daily Mail*, 23 February 1959, p. 6; The two leaders had a history of personal hostility and, according to Tony Benn, 'hated each other'. Benn, A. *Out of the wilderness: diaries, 1963–67*, p. 1.

CHAPTER THREE

1 *Daily Mail*, 5 March 1959, p. 11.

2 A. Gromyko, *Memories* (London, 1989), p. 157.

3 Statement to the House of Commons by the prime minister, Wednesday 4 March 1959: TNA, PRO, FO371/143438.

4 CC(59), 14th Conclusions, Minute 1, 4 March 1959: TNA, PRO, CAB128/33; a similar conclusion was put forward in widely circulated foreign office paper: 'What Kind of Meeting Should We Go For?', 6 March 1959 [TNA, PRO, FO371/145823] and to the Embassies in London (e.g., Record of Conversation between Minister of State, John Profumo, and Yugoslavian ambassador, 9 March 1959 [TNA, PRO, FO371/143439].

5 Macmillan diary, 4 March 1959: Peter Catterall, *The Macmillan diaries, volume 2*: (London, forthcoming).

6 Statement to the House of Commons by the prime minister, Wednesday 4 March 1959: TNA, PRO, FO371/143438.

7 Macmillan, *Riding the storm*, p. 637.

8 'Visit of the prime minister and foreign secretary to Paris, March 1959', CAB133/293.

9 Macmillan, *Riding the storm*, p. 637.

10 Bonn to foreign office, 4 February 1959: TNA, PRO, FO371/145775.

11 Record of meeting in Palais Schaumberg, Bonn, 12–13 March 1959: TNA, PRO, PREM11/2676.

12 Ibid. Jean Lacouture notes that Dulles's resignation was considered a 'disaster' by Adenauer (J. Lacouture, *De Gaulle: the ruler, 1945–70* [London 1991], p. 336).

13 Macmillan, *Riding the storm*, p. 640.

14 Foreign office tel. 1498 to Washington, 16 March 1959, TNA, PRO, PREM11/2685; FO tel. 414 to Washington, 20 January 1959: TNA, PRO, PREM11/2775.

15 'Macmillan talks, position paper,' undated: Eisenhower Library (Abilene), White House Central File (Confidential File), Subject Series 78, Dept. of State (March, 1959), Briefing Book, Macmillan visit (2).

16 S. Ambrose, *Eisenhower: the president* (New York, 1984), p. 534.

17 Telephone conversation with the president, 13 March 1959: Eisenhower Library (Abilene, Kansas), Herter Papers 10, presidential calls, 1959 (2).

18 Telephone conversation with General Goodpaster, 12 March 1959: Eisenhower Library (Abilene), Herter papers 10, presidential calls, 1959 (2).

19 Staff Notes, 14 March 1959: Eisenhower Library (Abilene) Whitman File, DDE Diary Series 39, Staff Notes, March 1–15, 1959 (1).

20 Telephone call from Dulles to president, 20 January 1959: Eisenhower Library (Abilene), Whitman File, DDE Diary 38, Telephone calls, January, 1959.

21 The British launched their Suez offensive a week before the US presidential elections. R. Hathaway, *Great Britain and the United States: special relations since world war two* (Boston, 1990), p. 45.

22 Sampson, Macmillan, pp 146–7; For example, Senator Hubert Humphrey about the Moscow visit: 'I think Prime Minister Macmillan really personalized what we mean when we say being firm on the one hand and being willing to negotiate on the other. [...] He represents British courage, British character and real leadership: and I want to commend him.' 9 March 1959: TNA, PRO, FO371/143438.

23 Staff notes, 14 March 1959: Whitman File, DDE Diary 39, Staff notes, March 1–15, 1959 (1)

24 Memorandum of conference with the president, 20 March 1959: Eisenhower Library, Whitman File, International Series 22, Macmillan Visit, 20–22 March 1959 (4).

25 On the Berlin blockade, see: R. Edmonds, *Setting the mould: the United States and Britain, 1945–50* (New York, 1986), pp 178–81.

26 In fact, on 26 March the British ambassador in Moscow handed the Soviets an official reply to their note of 2 March that set progress at foreign ministers level as a necessary requirement to fixing a date for the summit. The Soviets responded on 30 March that they considered fixing a date for the summit immediately as the best way of ensuring success at the foreign ministers meeting, but to Macmillan's great relief, they agreed to attend the talks in Geneva. Moscow tel. 562 to foreign office, 31 March 1959: TNA, PRO, PREM11/2685; *Macmillan, Riding the storm*, p. 645

27 Memorandum of conference with the president, 20 March 1959: Eisenhower Library, Whitman File, International Series 22, Macmillan Visit, March 20–22, 1959 (4).

28 A. Horne, *Macmillan, volume 1, 1984–1956* (London, 1986), p. 135.

29 Memorandum of conference with the president, 20 March 1959: Eisenhower Library, Whitman File, International Series 22, Macmillan Visit, March 20–22, 1959 (4).

30 A. Horne, *Macmillan, volume 2, 1957–86* (London, 1989), pp 130, 134.

31 R. Blake, *The Conservative party from Peel to Thatcher* (London, 1985), p. 282.

32 State Dept. tel. 4861 from London, 3 April 1959: NA (College Park), State Department Decimal File 1955–59, RG59, 741.00.

33 State Dept. tel. 938 from London, 25 April 1959: NA (College Park), State Department Decimal File 1955–59, RG59, 741.00.

34 Ibid.

35 Record of conversation between the prime minister and Soviet ambassador, 8 April 1959: TNA, PRO, PREM11/2685.

36 Ambrose, *Eisenhower: the president*, p. 525.

37 The fullest daily account of the proceedings at Geneva can be found in: 'Geneva foreign ministers conference': NA (College Park), Department of State Lot Files, 64D291 Boxes 1–4

38 *Daily Mail*, May 12th, 1959, p. 1.

39 R. Rhodes James, *Anthony Eden* (London, 1986), pp 417–8.

40 405th Meeting of the National Security Council, 7 May 1959: Eisenhower Library (Abilene), Whitman File, NSC Series 11.

41 CC (59) 28th Conclusions, Minute 1, 5 May 1959: TNA, PRO, CAB128/33.

42 407th Meeting of the National Security Council, 21 May 1959: Eisenhower Library (Abilene), Whitman File, NSC Series 11.

43 Memorandum of Conversation, 22 May 1959: NA (College Park), Department of State Lot Files, 64D291.

44 *Daily Herald*, 3 June 1959, p. 1.

45 *Evening Standard*, 10 June 1959, p. 4.

46 State Dept. tel. 10647 to London, 3 June 1959: Eisenhower Library (Abilene), Whitman File, International Series 22, Macmillan, March 23rd–June 30, 1959 (4).

47 Macmillan, *Pointing the way*, p. 69.

48 D. Eisenhower, *The White House years: waging peace, 1956–61* (London, 1966), p. 401.

49 State Dept. tel. 10996 to London, 16 June 1959: Eisenhower Library (Abilene), Whitman File, International Series 22, Macmillan, March 23–June 30, 1959 (4).

50 Washington tel. 1427 to foreign office, 17 June 1959: TNA, PRO, FO371/145490; M. Beschloss, *Kennedy v. Khrushchev: the crisis years, 1960–63* (London, 1991), pp 193–225; State Dept. tel. 114 to Geneva, 16 June 1959: Eisenhower Library (Abilene), White House Staff Secretary, Subject Series, State Dept. sub-series 5, Geneva cables (1) – Supported by Revised draft of proposed message from president to Khrushchev, 15 June 1959: Eisenhower Library (Abilene), Whitman File, Dulles/Herter Series 9, Herter, secretary of state, June 1959 (2).

51 State Dept. tel. 6644 from London, 19 June 1959: NA (College Park), State Dept. Decimal File 1955–59, RG59 611.41.

52 State Dept. tel. 6672 from London, 22 June 1959: NA (College Park), State Dept Decimal File 1955–59, RG59 611.41.

53 Final revised draft of proposed message from president to Khrushchev, 15 June 1959: Eisenhower Library (Abilene), Whitman File, Dulles/Herter Series 9, Herter, secretary of state, June 1959 (2).

54 State Dept. tel. 114 to Geneva, 16 June 1959: Eisenhower Library (Abilene), White House Staff Secretary, Subject Series, State Dept. sub-series 5, Geneva cables (1).

55   Macmillan, *Pointing the way*, p. 71.
56   Ibid. pp 71–2.
57   Cabinet Conclusions 37, Minute 1, 23 June 1959: TNA, PRO, CAB128/33.
58   Foreign office tel. 2808 to Washington, 23 June 1959: TNA, PRO, FO371/145491.
59   Foreign office tel. 2811 to Washington, 23 June 1959: TNA, PRO, PREM11/2686.
60   Foreign office tel. 2840 to Washington, 25 June 1959: TNA, PRO, PREM11/2686.
61   Foreign office tel. 2843 to Washington, 25 June 1959: TNA, PRO, PREM11/2686.
62   Washington tel. 1475 to foreign office, 25 June 1959: TNA, PRO PREM11/2686.
63   Moscow tel. 949 to foreign office, 25 June 1959: TNA, PRO PREM11/2686.
64   Bonn tel. 645 to foreign office, 23 June 1959: TNA, PRO, FO371/145490.
65   Memorandum of Conversation with Adenauer, 27 May 1959: Eisenhower Library (Abilene), Herter Papers 21, Meetings with the president, 7 July 1957–1 January 1961
66   Record of Conversation between foreign secretary and French ambassador, 25 June 1959: TNA, PRO, FO371/145491.
67   Washington tel. 1475 to foreign office, 25 June 1959: TNA, PRO PREM11/2686.
68   Macmillan to Caccia, 26 June 1959: TNA, PRO, PREM11/2686.
69   Washington tel. 1486 to foreign office, 28 June 1959: TNA, PRO, PREM11/2686.
70   Macmillan to Caccia, 26 June 1959: TNA, PRO, PREM11/2686.
71   President to prime minister, 27 June 1959: TNA, PRO, PREM11/2686.
72   Foreign office tel. 2902 to Washington, 29 June 1959: TNA, PRO, PREM11/2686.
73   Memorandum of telephone conversation with the president, 8 July 1959: Eisenhower Library (Abilene), Herter Papers 10, presidential calls, 1959 (2).
74   Foreign Office tel. 2994 to Washington, 3 July 1959: TNA, PRO, PREM11/2686.
75   Record of conversation between Lloyd and Herter, 13 July 1959: TNA, PRO, PREM11/2686.
76   Ibid.
77   Macmillan, *Pointing the way*, p. 76.
78   Macmillan to Lloyd, 17 July 1959: TNA, PRO, PREM11/2686.
79   Eisenhower, *Waging peace*, p. 407.
80   Geneva tel. 311 to foreign office, 20 July 1959: TNA, PRO, PREM11/2686.
81   Foreign office tel. 569 to Geneva, 22 July 1959: TNA, PRO, FO371/145492.
82   Macmillan diary, 17 July 1959: Catterall, *Macmillan diaries, volume 2.*
83   Foreign office tel. 568 to Geneva, 22 July 1959: TNA, PRO, FO371/145492.
84   Foreign office tel. 576 to Geneva, 23 July 1959: TNA, PRO, PREM11/2686.
85   President to prime minister, 22 July 1959: TNA, PRO, PREM11/2686.
86   Macmillan diary, 23 July 1959: Catterall, *Macmillan diaries, volume 2.*

87   Foreign office tel. 576 to Geneva, 23 July 1959: TNA, PRO, PREM11/2686.
88   Foreign office tel. 581 to Geneva, 23 July 1959: TNA, PRO, PREM11/2686.
89   Lasky to de Zuleta, 23 July 1959: TNA, PRO, PREM11/2686.
90   Geneva tel. 338 to foreign office, 23 July 1959: TNA, PRO, FO371/145493.
91   Ibid. John Killick, Head of the FO Western Dept. minuted: 'There was never any chance of "extracting a price for a summit" since it has been obvious all along that we favoured a summit whatever happened.'
92   Geneva tel. 340 to foreign office, 23 July 1959: TNA, PRO, PREM11/2686.
93   Geneva tel. 340 to foreign office, 23 July 1959: TNA, PRO, PREM11/2686.
94   Record of Conversation between Lloyd and Herter, 24 July 1959: TNA, PRO, PREM11/2686.
95   Ibid.
96   Macmillan, *Pointing the way*, p. 78.
97   Foreign office tel. 585 to Geneva, 24 July 1959: TNA, PRO, PREM11/2686.
98   Macmillan, *Pointing the way*, pp 78–9.
99   Foreign office tel. 585 to Geneva, 24 July 1959: TNA, PRO, PREM11/2686.
100 Macmillan, *Pointing the way*, pp 79–80.
101 Draft message from prime minister to president, 28 July 1959: TNA, PRO, PREM11/2686.
102 State Dept. tel. 175 from Geneva, 27 July 1959: NA (College Park), State Dept. Decimal File, 1955–59, RG59, 611.41.
103 Geneva tel. 360 to foreign office, 28 July 1959: TNA, PRO PREM11/2686.
104 Geneva tel. 367 to foreign office, 29 July 1959: TNA, PRO, PREM11/2686.
105 Ibid.
106 Foreign office tel. 631 to Geneva, 29 July 1959: TNA, PRO, PREM11/2686.

CHAPTER FOUR

1   H. Macmillan, *Pointing the way* (London, 1972), p. 79.
2   S. Ambrose, *Eisenhower: the president* (New York, 1984), p. 536.
3   Macmillan, *Pointing the way*, p. 80.
4   P. Cerny, *The politics of grandeur; ideological aspects of de Gaulle's foreign policy* (Cambridge, 1980), p. 273; Geneva tel. 389 to foreign office, 1 August 1959: Public Record Office (Kew), PREM 11/2686; foreign office tel. 3370 to Washington, 2 August 1959: TNA, PRO, FO 371/145493; Geneva tel. 397 to foreign office, 2 August 1959: TNA, PRO, FO 371/145493; Ambrose, *Eisenhower: the president*, p. 536.
5   Foreign office tel. 725 to Geneva, 4 August 1959: TNA, PRO, PREM 11/2990.
6   Geneva tel. 406 to foreign office, 3 August 1959: TNA, PRO, PREM 11/2990.
7   Macmillan, *Pointing the way*, p. 81.
8   *Daily Herald*, 4 August 1959, p. 1; *Daily Mail*, 4 August 1959, p. 1; *Evening Standard*, 4 August, 1959, p. 8; *Observer*, 9 August 1959, p. 5.
9   Foreign office tel. 706 to Geneva, 2 August 1959: TNA, PRO, FO 371/145493.
10   Ambrose, *Eisenhower: the president*, pp 534, 537.

11 Whitman diary, 7–15 August 1959: Eisenhower Library (Abilene, Kansas), Whitman File, Ann Whitman Diary Series 11, ACW August, 1959 (2).
12 Ambrose, *Eisenhower: the president*, p. 541.
13 *Daily Herald*, 27 August 1959, p. 1; Eisenhower, D. *Waging peace, 1956–61* (London, 1966), p. 419.
14 Eisenhower, *Waging peace*, p. 419.
15 *Evening Standard*, 27 August 1959, p. 1; *Daily Herald*, 28–9August 1959, p. 1; *Daily Mail*, 28–29 August 1959, p. 1.
16 Meeting with Eisenhower, 29 August 1959: TNA, PRO, FO 371/145494; Ambrose, *Eisenhower: the president*, p. 538.
17 A. Horne, *Macmillan, volume 2, 1957–86* (London, 1989), pp 147–8; Ambrose, *Eisenhower: the president*, p. 540; *Daily Herald*, 28 August 1959, p. 1.
18 From president to prime minister, 1 & 5 September 1959: Eisenhower Library (Abilene), Whitman File, International Series 23, Macmillan, 7/1/59–12/13/59 (6).
19 Macmillan, *Pointing the way*, p. 87.
20 Horne, *Macmillan, volume 2*, p. 147.
21 Memorandum of conversation with Lloyd, 19 October 1958: Eisenhower Library (Abilene), Dulles Papers, General Correspondence series 1, Memo of conversations, General L-M (1).
22 *Evening Standard*, 1 September 1959, p. 1; *Daily Herald*, 1 September 1959, p. 1; *Daily Mail*, September 1st, 1959, p. 1.
23 B. Bruce, *Images of power* (London, 1992), p. 31.
24 Macmillan diary, 31 August 1959: Catterall, *Macmillan diaries, volume 2*; Bruce, *Images of power*, p. 31; Horne, *Macmillan, volume 2*, p. 148; Seymour-Ure, C. *The British press and broadcasting since 1945* (Oxford, 1991), p. 185.
25 *Daily Mail*, 1 September 1959, p. 1; *Evening Standard*, 1 September 1959, p. 11; *Observer*, 6 September 1959, p. 16; *Daily Herald*, September 1st, 1959, p. 1.
26 Horne, *Macmillan, volume 2*, p. 148.
27 Bruce, *Images of power*, p. 31.
28 Legislative meeting, 8 September 1959: Eisenhower Library (Abilene), Whitman File, Legislative Meeting Series, Leg. Meetings, July-September 1959.
29 Telephone conversation with Cardinal Spellman, 9 September 1959: Eisenhower Library (Abilene), Whitman File, DDE Diary Series 45, Telephone Calls, September 1959; Eisenhower's proposals for private talks at Camp David apparently confused the Soviets. Khrushchev later recalled that 'I couldn't for the life of me find out what this Camp David was'. M. McCauley (ed.) *Khrushchev and Khrushchevism* (London, 1987), p. 181.
30 M. Beschloss, *Kennedy v. Khrushchev: the crisis years, 1960–63* (London, 1991), p. 211; McCauley, *Khrushchev and Khrushchevism*, pp 181–2.
31 Memorandum of Conversation with Khrushchev, 15 September 1959: NA (College Park), State Department Decimal File, 1955–59, RG59, 611.61.
32 Eisenhower, *Waging peace*, p. 439.

33 Ambrose, *Eisenhower: the president*, p. 542. Khrushchev initially refused to board the helicopter, suspecting a CIA assassination attempt. He only agreed to go on the trip when Eisenhower made it clear that he was coming too.

34 Ambrose, *Eisenhower: the president*, p. 542; L. May, (ed.) *Recasting America: culture and politics in the age of the cold war* (Chicago, 1989), p. 82.

35 Memorandum of conference with the president, 28 September 1959: Eisenhower Library (Abilene), Whitman File, DDE Diary Series 44, Staff Notes, September, 1959 (1)

36 A. Gromyko, *Memories* (London 1989), p. 169.

37 Memorandum of talks with Khrushchev at Camp David, undated: Eisenhower Library (Abilene), Whitman File, International Series 48, Khrushchev Visit (1).

38 Ibid.

39 Ibid.

40 Memorandum of conference with the president, 28 September 1959: Eisenhower Library (Abilene), Whitman File, DDE Diary Series 44, Staff Notes, September, 1959 (1).

41 M. Beschloss, *Mayday: Eisenhower, Khrushchev and the U2 affair* (London, 1986), pp 216–7.

42 Washington tel. 2068 to foreign office, 29 September 1959: TNA, PRO, PREM 11/2990.

43 Foreign office tel. 4275 to Washington, 30 September 1959: TNA, PRO, FO 371/145494.

44 Record of conversation between Hoyer Millar and ambassador Chauvel, 30 September 1959: TNA, PRO, FO 371/145494.

45 Washington tel. 2079 to foreign office, 30 September 1959: TNA, PRO, FO 371/145494.

46 Foreign office tel. 4288 to Washington, 1 October 1959: TNA, PRO, FO 371/145494.

47 Foreign office tel. 4287 to Washington, 1 October 1959: TNA, PRO, PREM 11/2990. The penultimate paragraph of this telegram has been deleted, as Hoyer Miller said it would be. The original letter is not to found in the declassified Herter files held by the Eisenhower Library (Abilene).

48 Washington tel. 2103 to foreign office, 2 October 1959: TNA, PRO, PREM 11/2990.

49 Ibid.

50 Ibid.

51 Morgan Phillips, Labour Party Press conference, 3 October 1959: TNA, PRO, PREM 11/2990.

52 D. Butler, & R. Rose, *The British general election of 1959* (London, 1960), p. 65.

53 Tomkins to Wilkinson, 2 October 1959: TNA, PRO, FO 371/145494.

54 1959 general election results: Conservatives, 365 seats; Labour, 258 seats; Liberals, 6 seats; Independents, 1 seat. Conservative majority: over Labour, 107; over all parties, 100. Conservatives won 49.4% of the vote.

55 H. Young, *One of us* (London, 1991), p. 41.

56 J. Young, *Cold war Europe, 1945–89* (London, 1991), p. 114.

57 Butler & Rose, *1959 General election*, p. 256.
58 State Dept. tel. 1328 from London, 9 September 1959: NA (College Park), State Dept. Decimal File, 1955–59, RG59, 741.00.
59 Butler & Rose, *1959 general election*, p. 71.
60 Ibid.
61 *Evening Standard*, 1 September 1959, p. 4.
62 R. Taylor, *Against the bomb: the British peace movement, 1958–65* (Oxford, 1988), pp 51–2.
63 Horne, *Macmillan, volume 2*, p. 152.
64 Butler & Rose, *1959 General election*, p. 189.
65 Macmillan, *Pointing the way*, p. 14.
66 A. Sampson, *Macmillan: a study in ambiguity* (London, 1967), p. 149.
67 Macmillan, *Pointing the way*, p. 17.
68 D.R. Thorpe, *Selwyn Lloyd* (London, 1989), p. 296; Macmillan, as much anyone, was surprised when this view did not prevail after the 'Night of the Long Knives'(Horne, *Macmillan, volume 2*, p. 344).
69 Thorpe, *Selwyn Lloyd*, p. 296.
70 State Dept. tel. 1548 to Paris, 9 October 1959: Eisenhower Library (Abilene), Whitman File, International Series 12, de Gaulle, 15 September 1959 (onwards).
71 Macmillan, *Pointing the way*, p. 93.
72 State Dept. tel. 1548 to Paris, 9 October 1959: Eisenhower Library (Abilene), Whitman File, International Series 12, de Gaulle, 15 September 1959 (onwards).
73 Ambrose, *Eisenhower: the president*, p. 534.
74 For example, during the Cuban missile crisis (Beschloss, *Kennedy v. Khrushchev*, p. 478).
75 A. Grosser, *The western alliance* (London, 1980), pp 184–5.
76 Harrison, *The reluctant ally*, pp 63–5.
77 C. de Gaulle, *Memoirs of hope: renewal 1958–62, endeavour 1962–* (London, 1971), pp 201–2; Grosser, *The western alliance*, pp 166–7; Cerny, *The politics of grandeur*, pp 168–75.
78 J. Lacouture, *De Gaulle: the ruler, 1945–70* (London, 1991), pp 368–9.
79 Cerny, *Politics of grandeur*, p. 167. At the highest level, opposition to aiding the French nuclear programme was led by secretary of state, Herter; Lacouture, *De Gaulle: the ruler*, pp 368–9
80 Washington tel. 2153 to foreign office, 9 October 1959: TNA, PRO, PREM 11/2996; Lacouture, *De Gaulle: the ruler*, pp 369, 390, 416–17.
81 Foreign office tel. 1552 to Paris, 21 October 1959: TNA, PRO, PREM 11/2990.
82 Paris tel. 307 to foreign office, 20 October 1959: TNA, PRO, PREM 11 2996. This perception of an American 'lag', used to devastating effect by Kennedy in the 1960 election, was, in fact, completely spurious (Beschloss, *Kennedy v. Khrushchev*, pp 25–8).
83 Meeting with ambassador Chauvel, 21 October 1959: TNA, PRO, FO 371/145497.

84 Paris tel. 309 to foreign office, 21 October 1959: TNA, PRO, PREM 11/2990.

85 M. Jones, *The limits of liberty* (London, 1983), p. 535; Beschloss, *Kennedy v. Khrushchev*, p. 21.

86 Memorandum of conference with the president, 27 October 1959: Eisenhower Library (Abilene), Whitman File, DDE Series 45, Staff notes, October, 1959 (1).

87 Memorandum of conference with the president, 27 October 1959: Eisenhower Library (Abilene), Whitman File, DDE Series 45, Staff notes, October, 1959 (1).

88 Beschloss, *Mayday*, p. 219; Nogee & Donaldson, *Soviet foreign policy*, p. 115; Ambrose, *Rise to globalism*, pp 171–2.

89 Memorandum of conference with the president, 16 October 1959: Eisenhower Library (Abilene), Whitman File, DDE Series 45, Staff notes, October, 1959 (1).

90 Washington tel. 2222 to foreign office, 20 October 1959: TNA, PRO, FO 371/145496.

91 Memorandum of conference with the president, 27 October 1959: Eisenhower Library (Abilene), Whitman File, DDE Series 45, Staff notes, October, 1959 (1).

92 Foreign office tel. 4487 to Washington, 16 October 1959: TNA, PRO, FO 371/145495.

93 Foreign office tel. 4651 to Washington, 28 October 1959: TNA, PRO, FO 371/145497.

94 Macmillan diary, 29 October 1959: Catterall, *Macmillan diaries, volume 2*.

95 Commonwealth Relations Office tel. 1060 to Canberra, 10 November 1959: TNA, PRO, FO 371/145499.

96 Macmillan, *Pointing the way*, p. 104; Horne, *Macmillan, volume 2*, p. 219; Record of meetings in Paris, 19 December 1959: TNA, PRO, PREM 11/2991.

97 Macmillan, *Pointing the way*, p. 102.

98 Ibid. p. 104; Horne, *Macmillan, volume 2*, p. 219; Record of meetings in Paris, 19 December 1959: TNA, PRO, PREM 11/2991.

99 Macmillan, *Pointing the way*, p. 104; Horne, *Macmillan, volume 2*, p. 219; Record of meetings in Paris, 19 December 1959: TNA, PRO, PREM 11/2991.

100 Macmillan, *Pointing the way*, pp 102–3, 114.

101 Paris tel. 393 to foreign office, 20 December 1959: TNA, PRO, PREM 11/2991.

102 Macmillan diary, 21 December 1959: Catterall, *Macmillan diary*, volume 2.

103 Macmillan to Lloyd, 'Paris conference, December 19th–21st, 1959', 22 December 1959: TNA, PRO, PREM 11/2996.

104 Lloyd to Macmillan, 31 December 1959: TNA, PRO, PREM 11/2996.

105 State Dept tel. 1728 from Moscow, 25 December 1959: NA (College Park), State Dept. Decimal File, 1955–59, RG59, 611.61; Moscow tel. 1757 to foreign office, 25 December, 1959: TNA, PRO, FO 371/145501.

106 Paris tel. 410 to foreign office, 28 December 1959: TNA, PRO, PREM 11/2991; Moscow tel. 1774 to foreign office, 30 December 1959: TNA, PRO, PREM 11/2991.
107 Macmillan diary, 30 December 1959: Catterall, *Macmillan diaries, volume 2*.

CHAPTER FIVE

1 Dean to foreign secretary, 15 March 1960: TNA, PRO FO 371/152133. The full report remains classified as *Top Secret*.
2 Hailsham to Macmillan, 16 February 1960: TNA, PRO, FO 371/152131.
3 Dean to foreign secretary, 15 March 1960: TNA, PRO FO 371/152133; *Defence and Economic Aid: The Resources Balance Sheet*, 2 December, 1959: TNA, PRO, T234/277.
4 Dean to foreign secretary, 15 March 1960: TNA, PRO FO 371/152133.
5 Ibid.
6 Macmillan to Lloyd, 22 October 1959: TNA, PRO, PREM 11/2985.
7 Lloyd to Macmillan, 13 December 1959: TNA, PRO, PREM 11/2985.
8 Lloyd to Macmillan, 15 February 1960: TNA, PRO, PREM 11/2998.
9 Ibid.
10 De Zulueta to prime minister, 27 October 1960: TNA, PRO, PREM 11/2985.
11 De Zulueta to prime minister, 27 October 1960: TNA, PRO, PREM 11/2985; Macmillan to Lloyd, 2 December 1959: TNA, PRO, PREM 11/2996; Note dictated by R.A. Butler, 15 March 1960: Trinity College, Papers of Lord Butler of Saffron Walden, RAB/G35.
12 Jebb to foreign secretary, 17 February 1960: TNA, PRO FO 371/153909.
13 Summary of talking points for Rambouillet, 8 March 1960: TNA, PRO, PREM 11/2998.
14 Points discussed with President de Gaulle at Rambouillet on 12–13 March, 1960: TNA, PRO, PREM 11/2998.
15 Macmillan, *Pointing the way*, p. 181.
16 Points discussed with President de Gaulle at Rambouillet on 12–13 March 1960: TNA, PRO, PREM 11/2998.
17 Macmillan, *Pointing the way*, p. 114.
18 Foreign office minute by P.F. Hancock, 14 February 1959: TNA, PRO, FO 371/145819.
19 Horne, *Macmillan, volume 2*, p. 222.
20 Prime minister to the Queen, 14 March 1960: TNA, PRO, PREM 11/2998.
21 Address by President de Gaulle to Members of both Houses of Parliament at Westminster Hall, 7 April 1960: TNA, PRO, FO 371/153913.
22 Horne, *Macmillan, volume 2*, p. 223.
23 Jebb to Lloyd, 8 April 1960: TNA, PRO, FO 371/153914.
24 Record of conversation between Hoyer Millar and the French ambassador, 12 February 1960: TNA, PRO, FO 371/153905.
25 Conversation between President de Gaulle and prime minister, 5 April 1960: TNA, PRO, PREM 11/2978.

26 Macmillan, H. *Riding the storm, 1956–59* (London, 1971), p. 633. This was, of course, not true. Nevertheless, Macmillan's lack of awareness about Kremlin politics was not really his fault. Reilly's reviews and telegrams all suggested that Khrushchev had absolute authority, an impression compounded by the apparent servitude of foreign minister Andrei Gromyko. Moreover, as Sir Frank Roberts, ambassador in Moscow from 1960, has made clear, Khrushchev was such a powerful and ebullient personality that he seemed to 'set the tone' for everything. M. McCauley, *Khrushchev and Khrushchevism* (London, 1987), p. 221.

27 Conversations between President de Gaulle and prime minister, 5–6 April 1960: TNA, PRO, PREM 11/2978.

28 Ibid.

29 Macmillan diary, 13 March 1960: Peter Catterall, *Macmillan diaries, volume 2* (London, forthcoming).

30 CC (60), 19th Conclusions, 22 March 1960: TNA, PRO, CAB 128/34; the Soviets agreed to accept a treaty prohibiting all nuclear tests in the atmosphere, outer space or underwater. Underground tests above a seismic magnitude of 4.75 were also to be banned and joint research would be carried out to enable detection of explosions below that limit.

31 CC (60), 19th Conclusions, 22 March 1960: TNA, PRO, CAB 128/34.

32 Telephone conversation with Macmillan, 21 March 1960: Eisenhower Library (Abilene), Whitman File, DDE Series 48, Telephone Calls, March 1960.

33 Washington tel. 636 to foreign office, 23 March 1960: TNA, PRO, PREM 11/2994.

34 Lloyd to Macmillan, 24 March 1960: TNA, PRO, PREM 11/2994.

35 Telephone conversation with Eisenhower, 11 April 1960: Eisenhower Library (Abilene), Herter Papers 10, presidential Calls, January-June, 1960.

36 Macmillan diary, 28 March 1960: Catterall, *Macmillan diaries, volume 2* (forthcoming).

37 President to prime minister, 18 March, 1960: Eisenhower Library (Abilene), Whitman File, International Series 23, Macmillan, 1 January–4 August 1960 (7).

38 Notes on the prime minister's visit to Washington, undated [26 March 1960]: TNA, PRO, PREM 11/2994.

39 Macmillan diary, 13 March 1960: Catterall, *Macmillan diaries, volume 2* (forthcoming).

40 Macmillan, *Pointing the way*, p. 191.

41 p. 189.

42 Conversation with the president, 28 March 1960: TNA, PRO, PREM 11/2994.

43 Macmillan, *Pointing the way*, p. 189.

44 Washington Tels. 82 & 86 to foreign office, 29 March 1960: TNA, PRO, PREM 11/2994.

45 Eisenhower had offered Macmillan the chance to buy Polaris submarine-launched missiles, which the prime minister turned down. Britain had been warned about development problems with Skybolt. These problems and the

reduced vulnerability offered by a submarine force should have made Polaris the logical option. When Robert McNamara, US Secretary of Defence, cancelled the Skybolt programme in November 1962, only the personal intervention of President Kennedy secured Polaris for Britain as a replacement. See D. Murray, *Kennedy, Macmillan and nuclear weapons* (Basingstoke, 2000), and her essay in Richard Aldous and Sabine Lee (eds), *Harold Macmillan: aspects of a political life* (Basingstoke, 1999). See also S.J. Ball, *The bomber in British strategy* (Westview, 1995).

46 Prime minister to president, 31 March 1960: TNA, PRO, PREM 11/2994.

47 Jebb, 'Mr Khrushchev's Visit to France', 3 April 1960: TNA, PRO, FO 371/153901.

48 Beschloss, *Mayday*, pp 227–9.

49 Henderson to Rumbold, 3 April 1960: TNA, PRO, FO 371/151296; For example: Cambridge to Rumbold, 28 March, 1960: TNA, PRO, FO 371/151300; Rumbold to Murray, 29 March 1960: TNA, PRO, FO 371/151300.

50 Macmillan to Lloyd, 15 April 1960: TNA, PRO, FO 371/153780.

51 Foreign office tel. 1660 to Washington, 19 April 1960: TNA, PRO, FO 371/153780.

52 President to prime minister, March 18th, 1960: Eisenhower Library (Abilene), Whitman File, International Series 23, Macmillan, 1 January–4 August 1960 (7).

53 De Gaulle, *Memoirs of hope*, p. 243; Memorandum of Conversation between President Eisenhower and President de Gaulle, 25 April, 1960: Eisenhower Library (Abilene), Whitman File, International Series 12, de Gaulle visit to US, 22–25 April 1960 (1).

54 Ambrose, *Eisenhower: the president*, p. 570.

55 Ibid. p. 570; Beschloss, *Mayday*, pp 207–8.

56 Beschloss, *Mayday*, p. 240; Hood to Tomkins, 28 April 1960: TNA, PRO, FO 371/153902.

57 Meeting of the foreign ministers of USA, Britain and France, April 12th, 1960: TNA, PRO, FO 371/153784.

58 Discussions in preparation for the Paris Summit conference, 12–14 April 1960, volume 1: TNA, PRO, FO 371/153784.

59 Brief on Germany and Berlin for the foreign ministers meeting on 13 April 1960: TNA, PRO, FO 371/153783; See also briefs on disarmament, and East/West relations, TNA, PRO, FO 371/153783.

60 Bishop had been replaced as principal private secretary by Timothy Bligh in early 1960. He was transferred to the cabinet office and remained a key adviser to the prime minister.

61 Prime minister to Bishop, 21 April 1960: TNA, PRO, PREM 11/2992.

62 Eisenhower, *Waging peace*, p. 543; In the remaining pages of this chapter, the focus moves away from Macmillan to Eisenhower and the unfolding events of the U–2 incident. The crisis, which followed the shooting down of an American spy plane in Soviet airspace, dominated discussion in Paris later that month and is essential to an understanding of events at the summit.

63 A U–2 aircraft is on display at RAF Duxford in Cambridgeshire.

64 This background section on the development of the U–2 draws on chapters 3, 4 & 5 of Michael Beschloss's *Mayday*. Much of the detail about the U–2 incident is taken from that book and is footnoted accordingly. See also William Taubman, *Khrushchev: the man and his era* (New York, 2002).

65 Beschloss, *Mayday*, pp 14–16; Eisenhower, *Waging peace*, p. 547.

66 Beschloss, *Mayday*, p. 237.

67 'Eisenhower and his time' conference, Institute of US and Canadian Studies, Moscow, October 1990. (I am grateful to Professor M. M. Narinsky of the Russian Academy of Sciences for providing me with a transcript of this conference.)

68 'Eisenhower and his time' conference, Institute of US and Canadian Studies, Moscow, October 1990.

69 Beschloss, *Mayday*, pp 237–8.

70 Ibid., p. 239.

71 'Eisenhower and his time' conference, Institute of US and Canadian Studies, Moscow, October 1990.

72 Beschloss, *Mayday*, pp 42–4.

73 Ibid., pp 43–4.

74 Transcript of Press and Radio News Briefing, State Department, May 5th, 1960: Herter Papers 20, U–2 (1).

75 Beschloss, *Mayday*, p. 52.

76 Ibid., pp 53–4.

77 Ibid., pp 59–61; Moscow tel. 590 to foreign office, 9 May 1960: TNA, PRO, FO 371/151995.

78 Beschloss, *Mayday*, pp 59–61; Moscow tel. 590 to foreign office, 9 May 1960: TNA, PRO, FO 371/151995.

79 Beschloss, *Mayday*, p. 54.

80 Ibid. p. 257.

81 Diary, 9 May 1960: Eisenhower Library (Abilene), Whitman File, Whitman Diary Series 11, ACW Diary, May 1960.

82 New York Times Summary, 9 May 1960: Eisenhower Library (Abilene), White House Files (Staff Secretary), L. Arthur Minnich Series 16, NY Times Summaries, May 1960.

83 Diary, 9 May 1960: Eisenhower Library (Abilene), Whitman File, Whitman Diary Series 11, ACW Diary, May 1960.

84 Record of Actions by the National Security Council at its 44th Meeting, 9 May 1960: National Archives (Washington D.C.), National Security Actions 1952–60; Beschloss, *Mayday*, p. 255.

85 Ibid.

86 Telephone conversation with Nixon), 8 May 1960: Eisenhower Library (Abilene), Herter Papers 12, CAH Telephone Calls, 28/3/60 – 30/6/60.

87 Statement by the president, 11 May 1960: Eisenhower Library (Abilene), Whitman File, International Series 11, Paris summit Meeting, May 1960 (1).

88 Beschloss, *Mayday*, p. 259.

CHAPTER SIX

1 A. Horne, *Macmillan, volume 2, 1957–86* (London, 1989), p. 204.
2 H. Macmillan, *Pointing the way, 1959–61* (London, 1972), p. 195.
3 Macmillan diary, 7 May 1960: Peter Catterall, *Macmillan diaries volume 2* (London, forthcoming).
4 Macmillan, *Pointing the way*, p. 201.
5 Macmillan diary, 7 May 1960: Catterall, *Macmillan diaries, volume 2* (forthcoming).
6 C. De Gaulle, *Memoirs of hope* (London, 1971), p. 247.
7 Horne, *Macmillan, volume 2*, p. 226.
8 De Zulueta to prime minister, 11 May 1960: Public Record Office (Kew), PREM 11/2992.
9 Reilly to Rumbold, 10 May 1960: TNA, PRO, PREM 11/2992.
10 Macmillan, *Pointing the way*, p. 202.
11 444th meeting of the National Security Council, 9 May 1960: Eisenhower Library (Abilene), Whitman File, NSC Series 12, 444th Meeting of the NSC.
12 *Daily Mail*, 7 May 1960, p. 1.
13 *The Times*, 9 May 1960, p. 13; The popular papers took little interest in the U–2 incident and its consequences for the Paris summit, being more interested in the wedding of Princess Margaret to Antony Armstrong-Jones (*Evening Standard, Daily Herald*, 5–7 May 1960).
14 M. Beschloss, *Kennedy v. Khrushchev: the crisis years, 1960–63* (New York, 1991), p. 69.
15 William Taubman, *Khrushchev: the man and his era* (New York, 2002), p. 447.
16 Record of conversation between Lloyd and Herter at the US embassy, 14 May 1960, in record of the heads of government meeting in Paris, May 1960 (hereafter, *Paris, May 1960*). TNA, PRO, PREM 11/2992.
17 Minute by the foreign secretary of a conversation with Herter at the US embassy, 14 May 1960, *Paris, May 1960*: TNA, PRO, PREM 11/2992; Thorpe, D. *Selwyn Lloyd* (London, 1989), pp 302–3.
18 Ibid, p. 273. .
19 Record of conversation between the prime minister and Khrushchev at the British embassy, 15 May 1960, *Paris, May 1960*: TNA, PRO, PREM 11/2992.
20 Beschloss, *Mayday*, p. 274.
21 William Taubman, *Khrushchev: the man and his era* (New York, 2002), p. 461.
22 De Gaulle, *Memoirs of hope*, p. 248.
23 Beschloss, *Mayday*, p. 277.
24 Lacouture, *De Gaulle, 1945–70*, p. 391; Paris tel. 169 to foreign office, 15 May 1960: TNA, PRO, PREM 11/2992.
25 Macmillan, *Pointing the way*, p. 203; Horne, *Macmillan, vol.2*, p. 227.
26 Record of meeting between the prime minister, President Eisenhower and President de Gaulle, 15 May 1960, *Paris, May 1960*: TNA, PRO, PREM 11/2992; Macmillan, *Pointing the way*, p. 203.
27 Record of meeting between the prime minister, President Eisenhower and President de Gaulle, 15 May 1960, *Paris, May 1960*: TNA, PRO, PREM 11/2992.

28 Eisenhower, *Waging peace*, p. 554.
29 Dulles once told the president that the latter's world stature and the former's diplomatic experience made them a formidable team. Eisenhower's son, John, later remarked that what Dulles had meant was that 'with your contacts and my brains, we can't miss'. Beschloss, Mayday, p. 95.
30 Beschloss, *Mayday*, p. 94.
31 Ambrose, *Eisenhower: the president*, p. 534.
32 Record of meeting between the prime minister, President Eisenhower and President de Gaulle, 15 May 1960, *Paris, May 1960*: TNA, PRO, PREM 11/2992.
33 Macmillan, *Pointing the way*, pp 203–4.
34 Ibid. p. 204.
35 Ibid.
36 Ibid. Record of meeting with President Eisenhower at the United States ambassador's Residence, 16 May 1960, *Paris, May 1960*: TNA, PRO, PREM 11/2992.
37 The leaders of the wartime allies would meet again in November 1990 to bring the second world war to its symbolic conclusion.
38 Record of meeting between the four leaders, 16 May 1960, *Paris, May 1960*: TNA, PRO, PREM 11/2992; Beschloss, *Mayday*, p. 284.
39 Beschloss, *Mayday*, p. 285.
40 Record of meeting between the four leaders, 16 May 1960, *Paris, May 1960*: TNA, PRO, PREM 11/2992.
41 Ibid.
42 Ibid.
43 Macmillan, *Pointing the way*, p. 205.
44 Beschloss, *Mayday*, p. 285.
45 Record of meeting between the four leaders, 16 May 1960, *Paris, May 1960*: TNA, PRO, PREM 11/2992.
46 De Gaulle, *Memoirs of hope*, pp 250–1.
47 Record of meeting between the four leaders, 16 May 1960, *Paris, May 1960*: TNA, PRO, PREM 11/2992.
48 Beschloss, *Mayday*, p. 287.
49 Record of meeting between the four leaders, 16 May 1960, *Paris, May 1960*: TNA, PRO, PREM 11/2992.
50 Ibid.
51 Beschloss, *Mayday*, p. 288; Record of meeting between the four leaders, 16 May 1960, *Paris, May 1960*: TNA, PRO, PREM 11/2992.
52 Record of meeting between the four leaders, 16 May 1960, *Paris, May 1960*: TNA, PRO, PREM 11/2992.
53 Beschloss, *Mayday*, p. 288.
54 Record of meeting between the four leaders, 16 May 1960, *Paris, May 1960*: TNA, PRO, PREM 11/2992.
55 Eisenhower, *Waging peace*, p. 556.
56 Beschloss, *Mayday*, p. 289–90.
57 H. Brogan, *The Pelican history of the United States of America* (London, 1986), p. 627.

58 Memorandum of conference with the president, 16 May 1960: Eisenhower Library (Abilene), Whitman File, DDE Diary Series 50, Staff Notes, May 1960: Beschloss, *Mayday*, p. 290.

59 Memorandum of conference with the president, 16 May 1960: Eisenhower Library (Abilene), Whitman File, DDE Diary Series 50, Staff Notes, May 1960: Beschloss, *Mayday*, p. 290.

60 Statement by President Eisenhower, 16 May 1960: TNA, PRO, PREM 11/2992.

61 Paris tel. 179 to foreign office, 16 May 1960: TNA, PRO, FO 371/153763.

62 Lacouture, *De Gaulle, 1945–70*, p. 370.

63 Thorpe, *Selwyn Lloyd*, pp 303–4.

64 Minute by the prime minister of conversation with President de Gaulle, 16 May 1960, *Paris, May 1960*: TNA, PRO, PREM 11/2992.

65 Macmillan, *Pointing the way*, p. 207; Minute by the prime minister of a conversation with President Eisenhower, 16 May 1960, *Paris, May 1960*: TNA, PRO, PREM 11/2992.

66 Ibid.

67 Macmillan, *Pointing the way*, p. 208; Ambrose, *Eisenhower: the president*, p. 579. A similar incident occurred during the Cuban Missile crisis (arguably the most dangerous crisis of the cold war period). When, on 22 October 1962, Dean Acheson arrived in Paris to win de Gaulle's support for US actions, he was told to 'tell your president that France supports him unreservedly. [...] We are beside you'. Lacouture, *De Gaulle, 1945–70*, p. 375.

68 Thorpe, *Selwyn Lloyd*, p. 304.

69 Record of conversation between the prime minister and Mr Khrushchev, 16 May 1960, *Paris, May 1960*: TNA, PRO, PREM 11/2992.

70 Ibid.

71 Ibid.

72 Ibid.

73 Horne, *Macmillan, volume 2*, p. 229.

74 Macmillan, *Pointing the way*, p. 208.

75 Agency report of an impromptu press conference given by Khrushchev in the Rue de Granule at 9:10am on 17 May 1960, *Paris, May 1960*: TNA, PRO, PREM 11/2992.

76 Macmillan diary, 21 May 1960. Catterall, *Macmillan diaries, volume 2* (forthcoming).

77 Record of meeting between Macmillan, Eisenhower and de Gaulle, 17 May 1960, *Paris, May 1960*: TNA, PRO, PREM 11/2992.

78 Macmillan, *Pointing the way*, p. 208.

79 Correspondence between President de Gaulle and the prime minister on 17 May 1960, *Paris, May 1960*: TNA, PRO, PREM 11/2992.

80 Record of meeting between Macmillan, Eisenhower and de Gaulle, 17 May 1960, *Paris, May 1960*: TNA, PRO, PREM 11/2992.

81 Beschloss, *Mayday*, p. 295.

82 Record of meeting between Macmillan, Eisenhower and de Gaulle, 17 May 1960, *Paris, May 1960*: TNA, PRO, PREM 11/2992.

83   Ibid.
84   Ibid.
85   Ibid.
86   Beschloss, *Mayday*, p. 296.
87   Record of meeting between Macmillan, Eisenhower and de Gaulle, 17 May 1960, *Paris, May 1960*: TNA, PRO, PREM 11/2992.
88   Ibid.
89   Ibid.
90   Ibid.
91   Ibid.
92   Ibid.
93   Ibid.
94   Beschloss, *Mayday*, p. 296.
95   Horne, *Macmillan, volume 2*, p. 231.
96   Record of Conversation between Lloyd and Gromyko, 17 May 1960, *Paris, May 1960*: TNA, PRO, PREM 11/2992.
97   Ibid.
98   J. Schick, *The Berlin crisis, 1958–62* (Philadelphia, 1971), pp 12–15.
99   Record of Conversation between Lloyd and Gromyko, 17 May 1960, *Paris, May 1960*: TNA, PRO, PREM 11/2992.
100   Macmillan, *Pointing the way*, p. 211.
101   Statement issued by the three Western heads of government, 17 May 1960, *Paris, May 1960*: TNA, PRO, PREM 11/2992.
102   Horne, *Macmillan, volume 2*, p. 231; H. Evans, *Downing Street diary: the Macmillan years, 1957–63* (London, 1983), p. 113.
103   Evans, *Downing Street diary*, p. 114.
104   *Daily Herald*, 19 May 1960, p. 1.
105   *Evening Standard*, 17 May 1960, p. 5.
106   *Daily Mail*, 18 May 1960, p. 1.
107   *Daily Mail*, 21 May 1960, p. 1.
108   *Observer*, 22 May 1960, p. 16.
109   Record of Conversation between the prime minister and Khrushchev, 18 May 1960, *Paris, May 1960*: TNA, PRO, PREM 11/2992.
110   Taubman, *Khrushchev*, p. 466–7
111   Meeting of Chiefs of State and heads of government, Memorandum of conversation between President Eisenhower, President de Gaulle and prime minister Macmillan, 18 May 1960: Eisenhower Library (Abilene), Whitman File, International Series 11, Paris summit, May 1960 (1).
112   Eisenhower's doctors were very concerned about the effect of the summit on his health. Beschloss, *Mayday*, p. 297.
113   Eisenhower to de Gaulle, 18 May 1960: Eisenhower Library (Abilene), Whitman file, International series 12, de Gaulle, September 1959 onwards (7).
114   Eisenhower to Macmillan, 18 May 1960: TNA, PRO, PREM 11/2992
115   Commonwealth Relations Office tel. 240 to Ottawa and Canberra, 19 May 1960: TNA, PRO, PREM 11/2997

116 Macmillan diary, 21 May 1960. Catterall, *Macmillan diaries, volume 2* (forthcoming).
117 Ibid.

EPILOGUE

1 *Herald Tribune*, 23 May 1960, p. 1. This chapter is based in part on an earlier essay, "Harold Macmillan and the art of personal diplomacy' in R. Aldous & S. Lee, *Harold Macmillan and Britain's world role* (Basingstoke and London, 1996).
2 Foreign office tel. 102 to Rome, 25 May 1960: TNA, PRO, FO 371/153766 This telegram was printed and given wide circulation.
3 Prime minister to foreign secretary, 24 May 1960: TNA, PRO, FO 371/152128.
4 Record of Actions, 445th Meeting of the NSC, 24 May 1960: National Archives of the United States (Washington), US National Security Council, National Security Actions, 1952–60.
5 Prime minister to foreign secretary, 24 May 1960: TNA, PRO, FO 371/152128.
6 R. Holland, *Pursuit of greatness: Britain and the world role, 1900–1970* (London, 1991), p. 279; Dean to foreign secretary, 15 March, 1960; TNA, PRO, FO371/152133
7 'What I envisage is a series of meetings, each one leading on to the next ... Even if a summit meeting was not to make any progress at all I would feel that it could nevertheless serve a useful purpose provided it led to a further conference'. Macmillan to Robert Menzies, Commonwealth Relations Office tel. 1060 to Canberra, 10 November, 1959: TNA, PRO, FO371/145499; Macmillan, *Pointing the way*, p. 102–3; Macmillan to Lloyd, 22 December, 1959, Lloyd to Macmillan 31st December, 1959: TNA, PRO PREM11/2996; Lloyd to Macmillan, 13 December, 1959: TNA, PRO, PREM11/2985; A. Grosser, *The Western alliance: European-American relations since 1945* (London, 1980), p. 187; M. Harrison, *The reluctant ally: France and Atlantic security* (London, 1981), pp 52–3.
8 Eisenhower to Macmillan, 5 September, 1959: Eisenhower Library (Abilene), Whitman File, International Series 23, Macmillan 1–12/59 (6); Jebb to Lloyd, 8th April, 1960: TNA, PRO, FO371/153914.
9 New York Times Summaries, May 1960: Eisenhower Library (Abilene), Minnich Series 16; Beschloss, *Mayday*, p. 249 & p. 273 Diary, 9th May, 1960: Eisenhower Library (Abilene), Whitman File, Whitman Diary Series 11; 444th meeting of the NSC, 9 May, 1960: Eisenhower Library (Abilene), Whitman File, NSC Series 12.
10 Macmillan, *Pointing the way*, pp 205 & 208; Memorandum of conference with the president, 16 May, 1960: Eisenhower Library (Abilene), Whitman File, DDE Diary Series 50, Staff Notes; Beschloss, *Mayday*, p. 290.
11 Record of meeting between the four leaders, 16 May, 1960: TNA, PRO, FO371/1714, *Paris, May 1960*; D. Eisenhower, *The White House years: waging peace, 1956–61* (London, 1961), p. 556; Beschloss, *Mayday*, p. 290; Eisenhower to de Gaulle, 18 May, 1960: Eisenhower Library (Abilene), Whitman File, International series 12.

12 Macmillan, *Pointing the way*, p. 195; Macmillan to Lloyd, 24 May, 1960: TNA, PRO, FO371/152128; 445th Meeting of the NSC, 24th May, 1960: NA (College Park), National Security Actions, 1952–60; Horne, *Macmillan, volume 2*, pp 113 & 233.

13 Horne, *Macmillan, volume 2*, pp 281–2; de Zulueta to Macmillan, 24 February, 1961: TNA, PRO, PREM11/3326.

14 Sampson, *Macmillan*, p. 221; Horne, *Macmillan, volume 2*, pp 292–300; *Macmillan, Pointing the way*, pp 335–9 & 348–53.

15 M. Beschloss, *Kennedy v. Khrushchev: the crisis years, 1960–63* (London, 1991), pp 224–5; Macmillan, *Pointing the way*, pp 356–9; Horne, *Macmillan volume 2*, pp 303–5; Kennedy to Macmillan, 10 June, 1961: TNA, PRO, PREM11/3328; CC(61), 30th conclusions, minute 6, 6th June, 1961: TNA, PRO CAB128/35; A. Schlesinger, *A thousand days: John F. Kennedy in the White House* (London, 1965), pp 339–341.

16 Horne, *Macmillan, volume 2*, pp 368 & 575–9. For a more critical assessment of the Kennedy/Macmillan relationship, see Nigel Ashton, *Kennedy, Macmillan and the cold war: the irony of interdependence* (Basingstoke, 2002).

17 Horne, Macmillan, volume 2, pp 368–70 & 378; D. Reynolds, *Britannia overruled: British policy and world power in the 20th century* (London, 1991), p. 214.

18 Horne, *Macmillan, volume 2*, pp 523 & 439; Schlesinger, *A thousand days*, pp 736–9; Reynolds, *Britannia overruled*, pp 214–15.

Index

by Brad Morrow

Index